Kindergarten
Fundamentals

Thinking Kids™
An imprint of Carson-Dellosa Publishing LLC
P.O. Box 35665
Greensboro, NC 27425 USA

ISBN 978-1-4838-1297-7

02-092167784

Table Of Contents

Table Of Contents

Ways to Enrich Learning

Kindergarten is an exciting and rewarding time for young children. It is when the foundation for academic success is built. Children discover that learning is fun, which makes them want to achieve. Kindergartners need a great deal of attention, have short attention spans, and show extremes in behavior. You must create a learning environment in which your child wants to explore, learn new concepts, and practice new skills.

Your kindergartner is learning at her own pace. Keep in mind that children mature and develop skills at different rates. Some kindergartners love pencil and paper tasks, while others would rather learn through building, putting together puzzles, or doing pretend and movement activities. Through observation of your child, you will discover the ways that she learns best. Be creative and adjust each task to meet the needs of your child.

Remember that young kindergartners are not learning academic skills, but they are also learning how to participate in groups and express their feelings. Their self-esteem is increasing, and they are beginning to understand their own uniqueness. Your kindergartner needs support, guidance, participation, and undivided attention. Therefore, the activities in this book are designed for you and your child to complete together.

Some ideas for activities and materials that will enhance your child's learning experience are suggested below.

LANGUAGE ARTS

The single most important skill that a child needs is literacy. This skill is important for success in school and later in life. You can do many things to encourage literacy.

1. **Read to your child every day.** Read every day for at least 15 minutes. This often becomes a favorite time of the day for both a child and his family. Use the recommended reading list on page 7 as a starting point for reading to your preschooler. Some things you can do before, during, and after reading with your child include the following:
   • Talk about pictures
   • Ask questions about the characters
   • Have your child guess what will happen next
   • Encourage your child to retell her favorite stories or favorite parts of a story
   • Have your child make up new endings for stories
   • Visit the library and let your child choose new books
   • Encourage "pretend reading" by allowing children to look at pictures and make up their own words.

Ways to Enrich Learning

2. **Encourage letter recognition.** Young children develop interest in reading and phonics by making observations about how adults use written language. Some activities include the following:
   - Point to letters in the environment, such as on cereal boxes, in your child's printed name, and in books and magazines
   - Help your child learn to match letters and make words
   - Play listening games by having your child identify words that begin with the same sound
   - Identify common sight words in the environment, such as *stop* and *walk*.

3. **Provide language arts materials.** Fill your child's environment with literacy materials. Suggested materials include:
   - Magnetic letters
   - Books, magazines, newspapers, and catalogs
   - Paper, pencils, crayons, and paints (Encourage children to experiment with making circles, squiggles, and lines.)
   - Children's music and recorded children's stories
   - Computer programs that emphasize language arts and literacy skills

MATH

Many toys and puzzles provide young children with early math learning experiences. Point out all of the ways that we use numbers and other math skills in our daily lives.

1. **Cook or garden together.** Not only are these special activities for families to share together, but they also offer numerous learning experiences. Children can gain these valuable skills:
   - Measuring
   - Numbers and counting ("Stir 10 times." or "Drop three seeds in each hole.")
   - Increased observation skills

2. **Provide mathematical materials and activities.** Fill your child's environment with math materials and activities. Suggested materials include:
   - Magnifying glasse
   - Blocks and other building materials
   - Magnets and magnetic numerals
   - Scale
   - Objects that sink or float (for bath and water play)
   - Calculator and toy cash register
   - Puzzles
   - Sorting, matching, and classifying games

Getting Started

As you begin your learning adventure with your kindergartner, help your child organize some special materials. Here is a list of things your child may need:

pencils	glue	paint	scrap paper
crayons	buttons	paintbrushes	construction paper
markers	tape	paint water cup	old newspapers
colorful chalk	play dough	paint shirt	safety scissors

Have your child decorate a box for storing her supplies, and encourage her to return the supplies when she is finished using them. That way, she will always know where everything is. Nothing gets lost when "picking up" becomes a habit.

As you work through this book, you may find that there are many things you would like to save. Be prepared. Make and decorate a special memory box with your child. Take a photograph of your child and place it on the top of a box. To protect the photograph, cover it with laminate or clear shelf paper. Have your child draw and color pictures all over the box. You can use a spray finish to protect the box from wear and tear. (Be sure to cover the photograph before applying the spray to the box.)

If possible, keep an audio recorder nearby. Children love playing with audio recorders and listening to their voices. In future years, listening to recordings of your preschooler talking, reading stories, and singing songs will be a wonderful way for you and your child to remember these experiences.

The Alphabet

Aa	Jj	Ss
Bb	Kk	Tt
Cc	Ll	Uu
Dd	Mm	Vv
Ee	Nn	Ww
Ff	Oo	Xx
Gg	Pp	Yy
Hh	Qq	Zz
Ii	Rr	

Numbers 0-20

0 = zero	11 = eleven
1 = one	12 = twelve
2 = two	13 = thirteen
3 = three	14 = fourteen
4 = four	15 = fifteen
5 = five	16 = sixteen
6 = six	17 = seventeen
7 = seven	18 = eighteen
8 = eight	19 = nineteen
9 = nine	20 = twenty
10 = ten	

Recommended Reading List

Alexander and the Terrible, Horrible, No Good, Very Bad Day by Judith Viorst

Are You My Mother? by P. D. Eastman

Brown Bear, Brown Bear, What Do You See? by Bill Martin Jr.

Catalina Magdalena Hoopensteiner Wallendiner Hogan Logan Bogan Was Her Name by Tedd Arnold

Chicka Chicka Boom Boom by Bill Martin Jr. and John Archambault

Chickens to the Rescue by John Himmelman

Chrysanthemum by Kevin Henkes

Click, Clack, Moo: Cows That Type by Doreen Cronin

Cross-Country Cat by Mary Calhoun

Curious George by H. A. Rey

Don´t Let the Pigeon Drive the Bus! by Mo Willems

Duck for President by Doreen Cronin

The Empty Pot by Demi

First Day Jitters by Julie Danneberg

Giant Children by Brod Bagert

Giggle, Giggle, Quack by Doreen Cronin

The Grouchy Ladybug by Eric Carle

Harold and the Purple Crayon by Crockett Johnson

Harry the Dirty Dog by Gene Zion

Hooway for Wodney Wat by Helen Lester

Horton Hatches the Egg by Dr. Seuss

How I Became A Pirate by Melinda Long

I Like Myself! by Karen Beaumont

If You Give a Mouse a Cookie by Laura Joffe Numeroff

Inch by Inch by Leo Lionni

Is Your Mama a Llama? by Deborah Guarino

The Kissing Hand by Audrey Penn

Madeline by Ludwig Bemelmans

Millions of Cats by Wanda Gag

Miss Spider´s Tea Party by David Kirk

No, David! by David Shannon

Not a Box by Antoinette Portis

Olivia by Ian Falconer

On Mother´s Lap by Ann Herbert Scott

One Fish, Two Fish, Red Fish, Blue Fish by Dr. Seuss

Peter Pepper´s Pet Spectacular by Betty Paraskevas

Pirates Don´t Change Diapers by Melinda Long

Polar Bear, Polar Bear, What Do You Hear? by Bill Martin Jr.

Puss in Boots by Charles Perrault

Richard Scarry´s Best Storybook Ever by Richard Scarry

Some Dogs Do by Jez Alborough

Stanley´s Party by Linda Bailey

Stellaluna by Janell Cannon

Stone Soup by Marcia Brown

The Three Little Wolves and the Big Bad Pig by Eugene Trivizas

The Tiny Seed by Eric Carle

The True Story of the 3 Little Pigs! by Jon Scieszka

There´s a Nightmare in My Closet by Mercer Mayer

Unlovable by Dan Yaccarino

The Very Hungry Caterpillar by Eric Carle

What Do You Do with a Tail Like This? by Steve Jenkins and Robin Page

Where the Sidewalk Ends: The Poems & Drawings of Shel Silverstein by Shel Silverstein

Where the Wild Things Are by Maurice Sendak

Straight Lines

Trace the line from each cat to its ball of yarn.

Line Practice

Trace the line from each baseball to the glove.

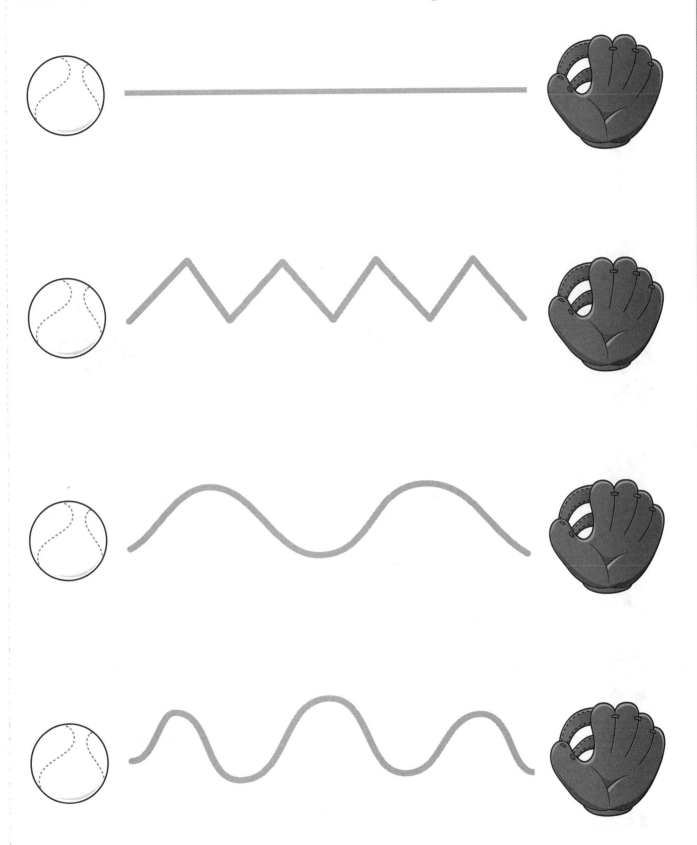

Follow The Path

Use a pencil to follow the path from each child to the toy.

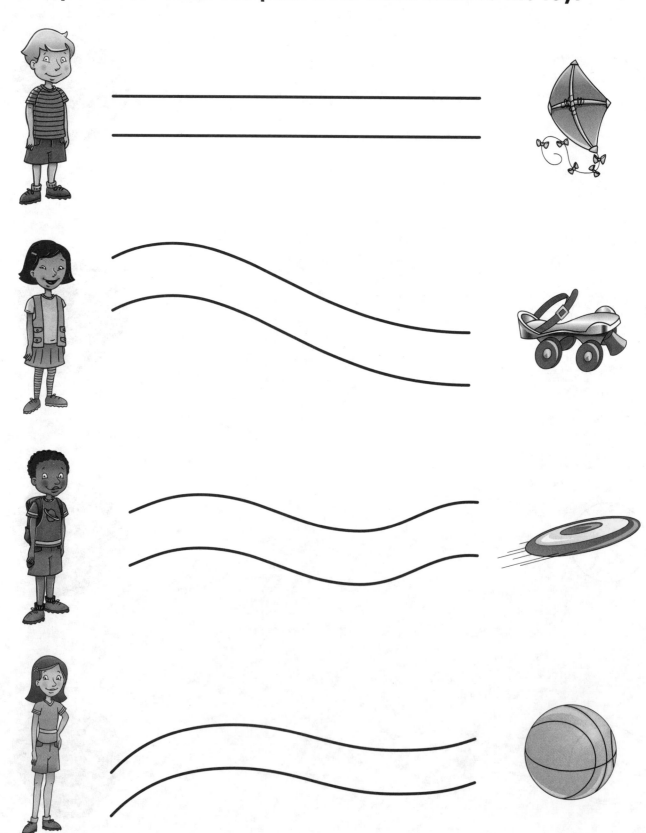

Follow The Path

Use a pencil to follow the path from each dog to its bone.

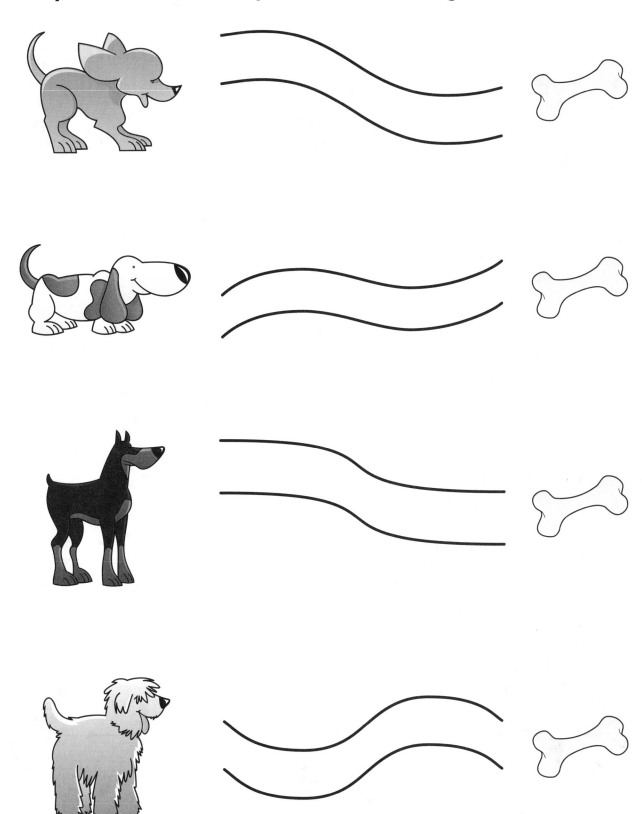

Top To Bottom

Trace each line from top to bottom.

Top To Bottom

Trace each line from top to bottom.

BOB'S BICYCLES

Follow The Path

Follow the path to help the race car win the race.

Follow The Path

Follow the path to help the horse find the barn.

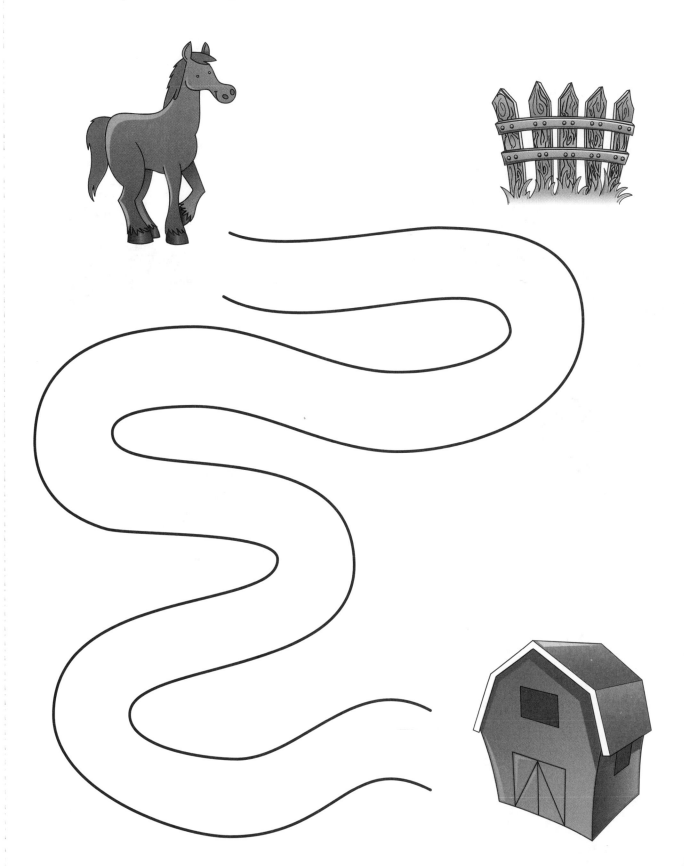

Hearts

Trace each heart on the dotted lines. Color each heart.

Flying Birds

Trace each bird on the dotted lines. Color each bird.

Falling Leaves

Trace each leaf on the dotted lines. Color each leaf.

Making Matches

Draw a line to connect each pair of matching objects.

Things That Are Different

Draw an X on the object that is different in each row.

Food Or Toy?

Circle each food item. Draw an X on each toy.

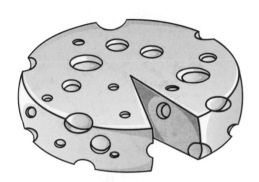

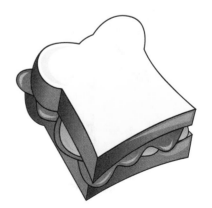

Animal Or Tree?

Circle each animal. Draw an X on each tree.

Little And Big

Draw a line from each big object to the small object that it matches.

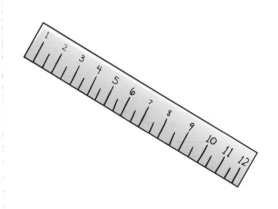

Little And Big

Circle each small object. Draw an X on each big picture.

Opposites

Draw a line from each picture to its opposite.

hard

night

left

down

day

soft

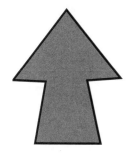

up

right

These Go Together

Draw a line to connect each pair of objects that go together.

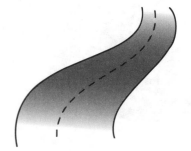

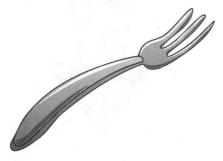

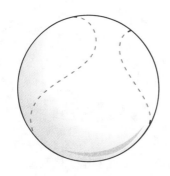
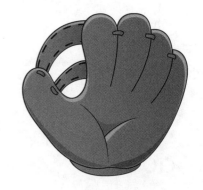

What Belongs?

Circle each object that you would find at the beach.

The Color Red

Color each object red. Say the name of each object as you color it.

apple

cherry

stop sign

strawberry

valentine

The Color Blue

Color each object blue. Say the name of each object as you color it.

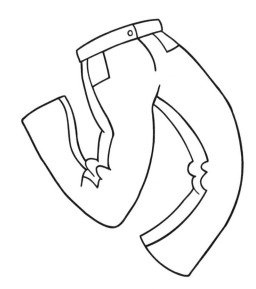

blue jeans

blue ribbon

crayon

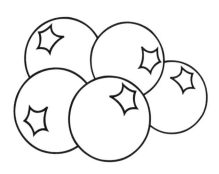

blueberries

bluebird

The Color Yellow

Color each object yellow. Say the name of each object as you color it.

banana

butter

sun

corn

chick

The Color Green

Color each object green. Say the name of each object as you color it.

tree

turtle

leaf

frog

grass

The Color Orange

Color each object orange. Say the name of each object as you color it.

carrot

basketball

pumpkin

goldfish

orange

The Color Purple

Color each object purple. Say the name of each object as you color it.

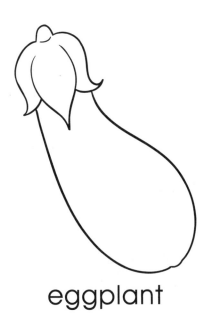

eggplant

grapes

purple crayon

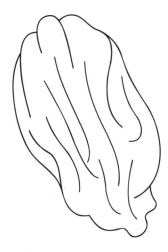

prune

violets

The Color Brown

Color each object brown. Say the name of each object as you color it.

chocolate

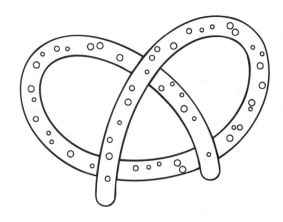

pretzel

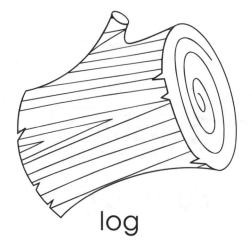

log

squirrel

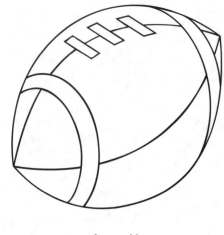

ball

The Color Black

Color each object black. Say the name of each object as you color it.

crow

bat

tire

piano

top hat

Same Colors

Color each object the correct color. Draw a line to connect each pair of objects that are the same color.

Same Colors

Color each object the correct color. Draw a line to connect each pair of objects that are the same color.

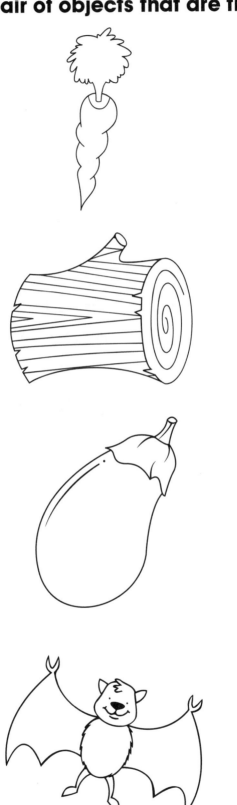
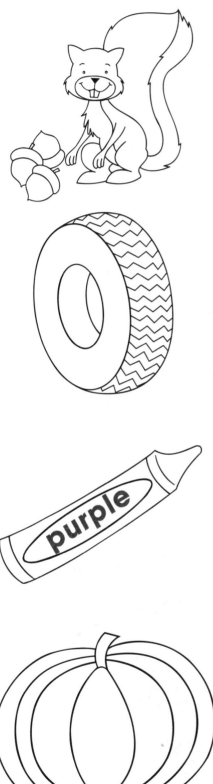

purple

Color Words

Color each paint can to match its color word.

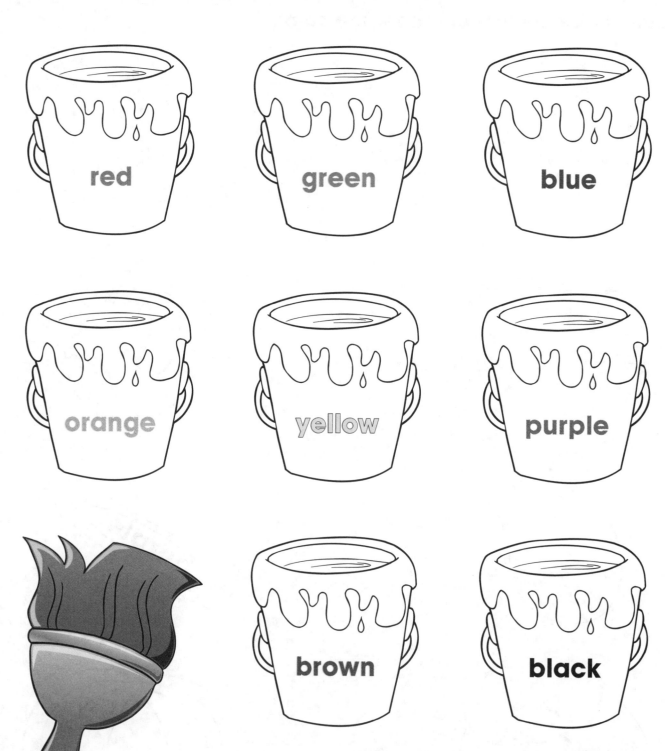

red

green

blue

orange

yellow

purple

brown

black

Shapes

Trace each shape. Say the name of each shape as you trace it. Color each shape.

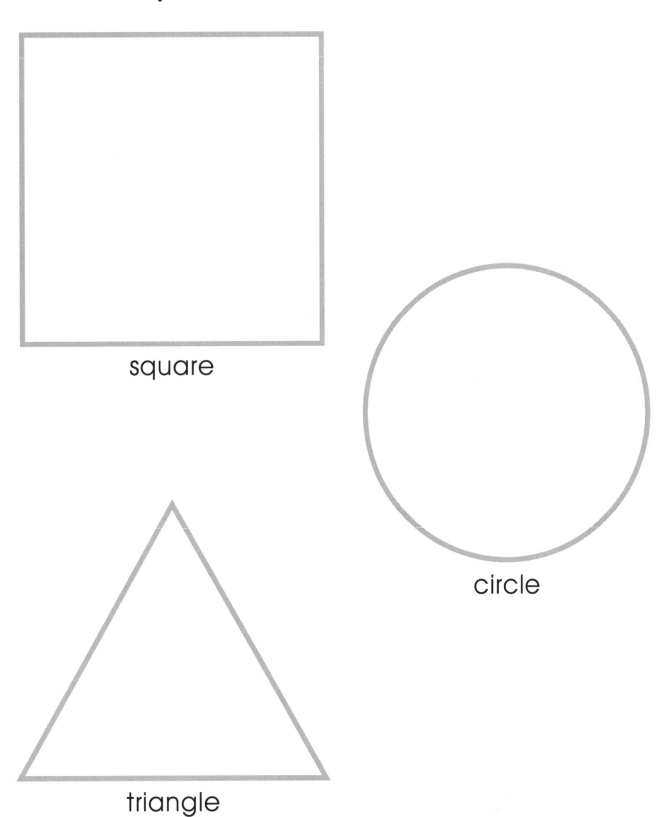

square

circle

triangle

Trace each shape. Say the name of each shape as you trace it. Color each shape.

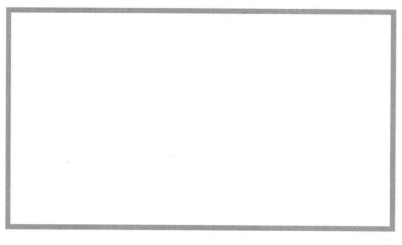

rectangle

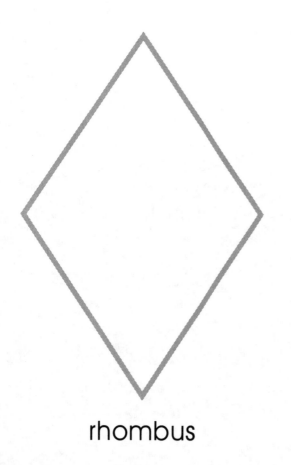

rhombus

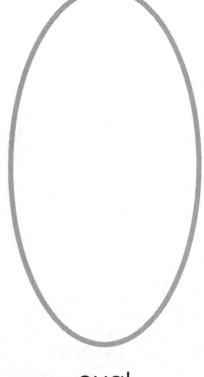

oval

Shapes

**Trace each shape. Say the name of each shape as you trace it.
Color each shape.**

square

circle

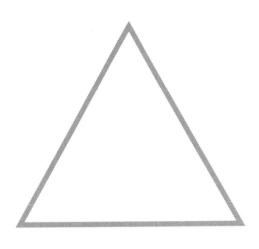

triangle

rhombus

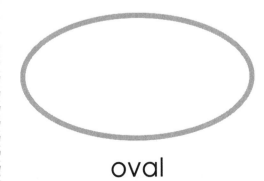

oval

rectangle

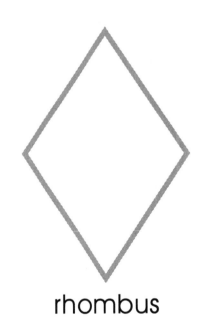

Same Shapes

Look at the first shape in each row. Color the shape that is the same in the row.

X Marks The Difference

Draw an X on the shape that is different in each row.

Patterns

Look at the pattern in each row. Draw the shape that comes next.

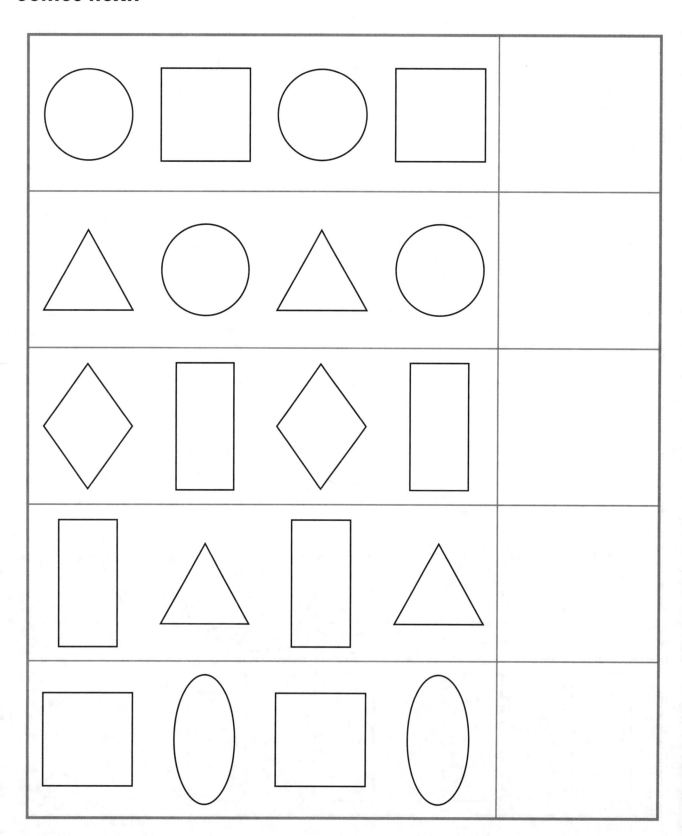

Patterns

Look at the pattern in each row. Draw the shape that comes next.

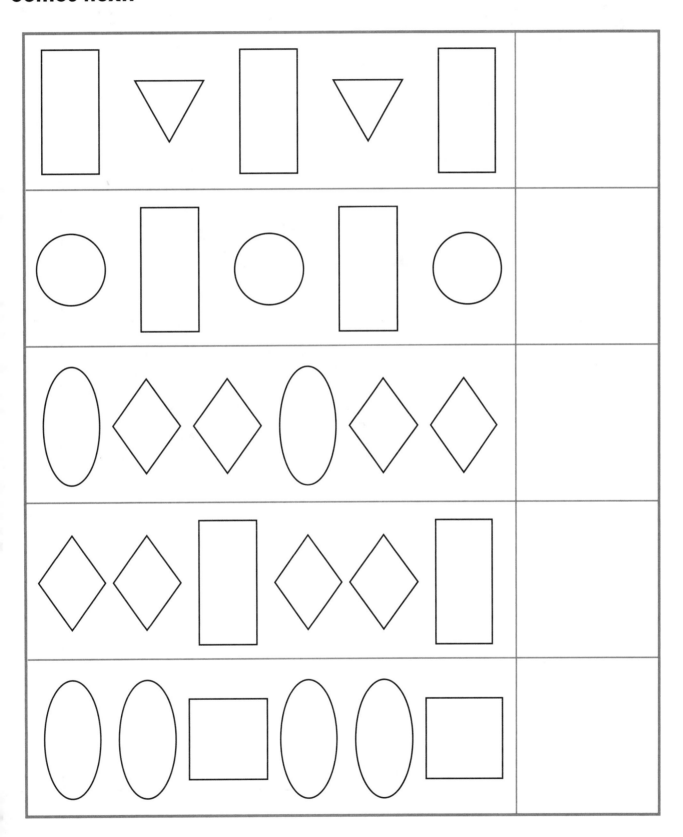

Hidden Picture

Use the code to color the spaces and find the hidden picture.

■ = yellow   ● = orange   ▲ = blue

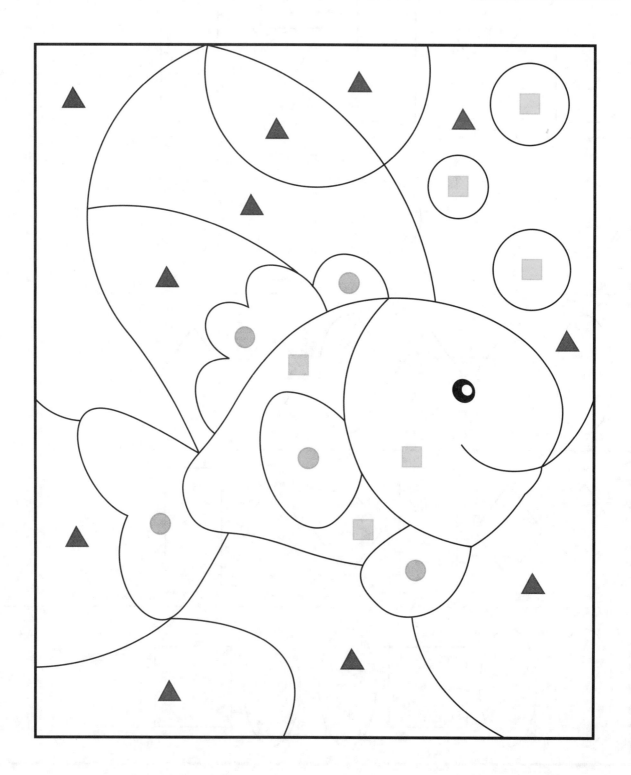

Hidden Picture

Use the code to color the spaces and find the hidden picture.

■ = **blue**   ★ = yellow

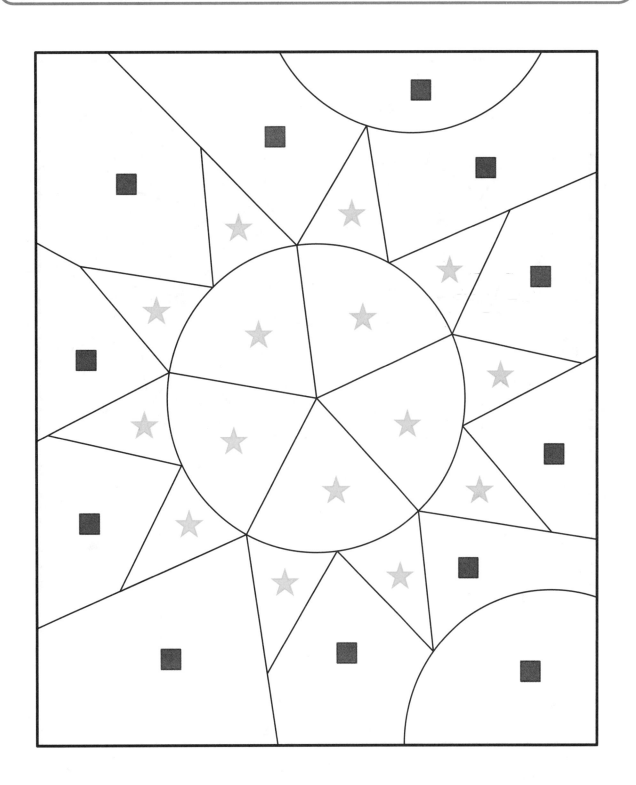

Hidden Picture

Use the code to color the spaces and find the hidden picture.

◆ = pink   ● = green

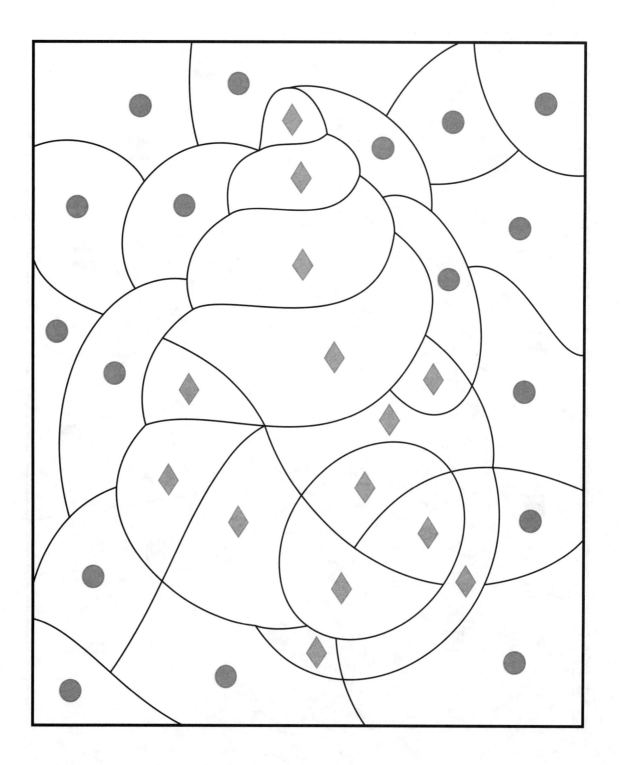

Hidden Picture

Use the code to color the spaces and find the hidden picture.

▲ = **blue**   ⬤ = yellow

Hidden Picture

Use the code to color the spaces and find the hidden picture.

● = **blue**   ■ = **red**   ▲ = yellow   ◆ = **green**

Hidden Picture

Use the code to color the spaces and find the hidden picture.

◆ = **green**   ● = **blue**

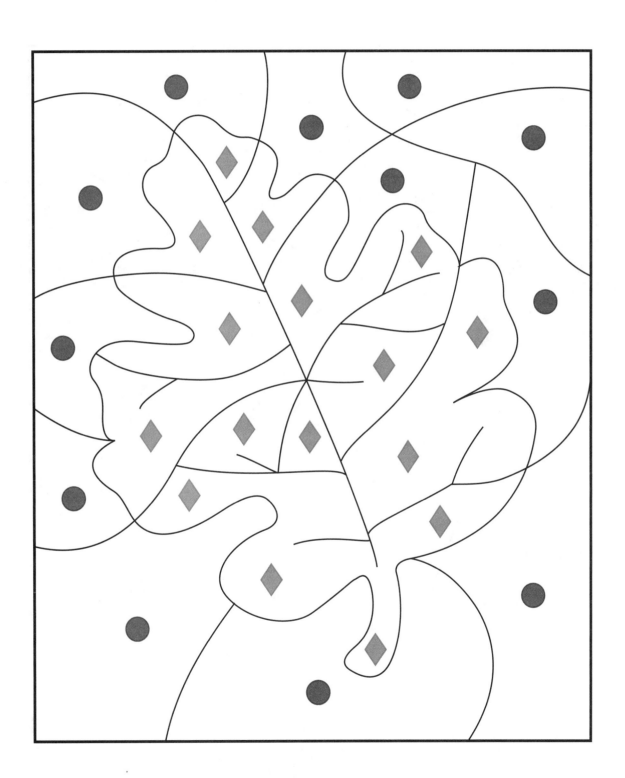

Hidden Picture

Use the code to color the spaces and find the hidden picture.

● = yellow ■ = brown ▲ = red ◆ = blue

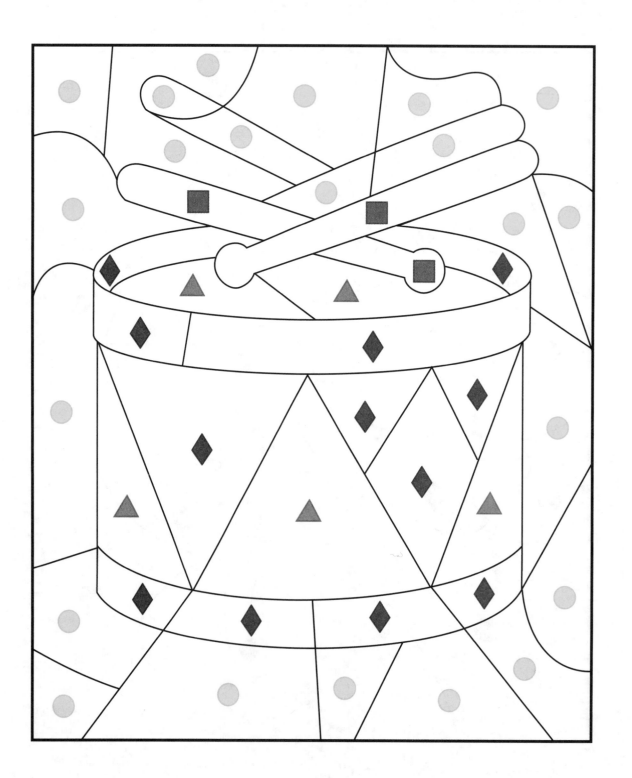

The Alphabet

A B C D E F G

H I J K L M N

O P Q R S T

U V W X Y Z

a b c d e f g h i j k l m n

o p q r s t u v w x y z

Uppercase Letter A

Trace each letter. Write the letter on the lines. Color the picture.

Lowercase Letter A

Trace each letter. Write the letter on the lines. Color the picture.

a a

a a

a a

a

Uppercase Letter B

Trace each letter. Write the letter on the lines. Color the picture.

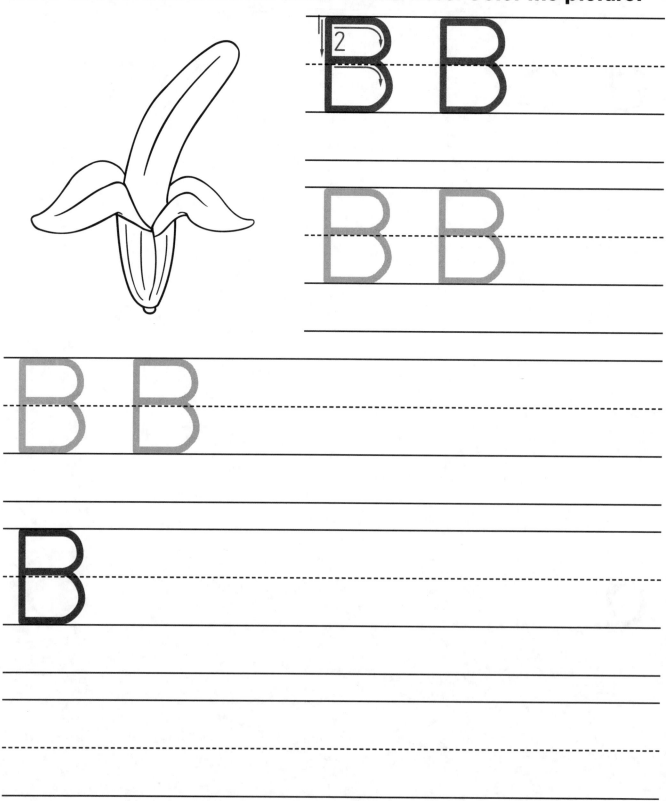

Lowercase Letter B

Trace each letter. Write the letter on the lines. Color the picture.

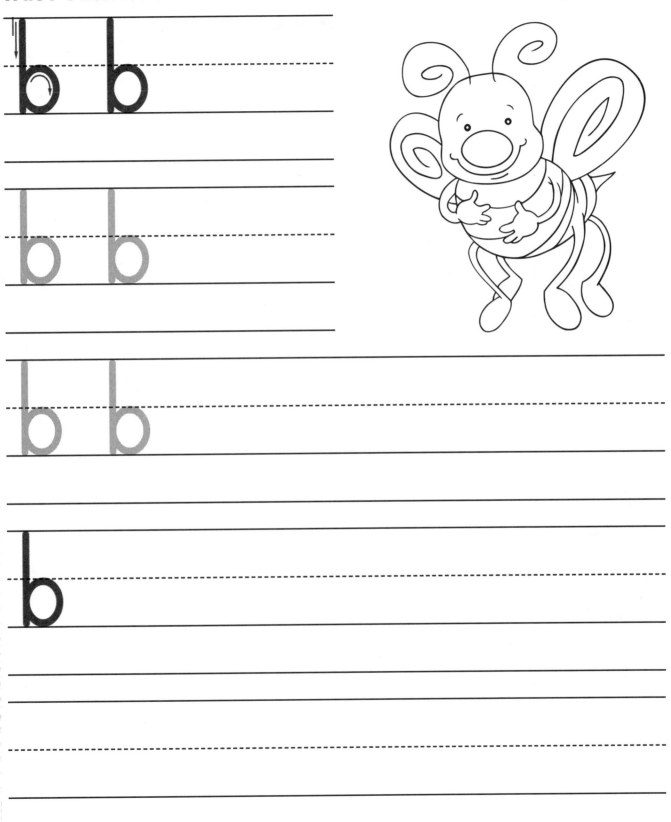

Uppercase Letter C

Trace each letter. Write the letter on the lines. Color the picture.

Lowercase Letter C

Trace each letter. Write the letter on the lines. Color the picture.

C C

C C

C C

C

Uppercase Letter D

Trace each letter. Write the letter on the lines. Color the picture.

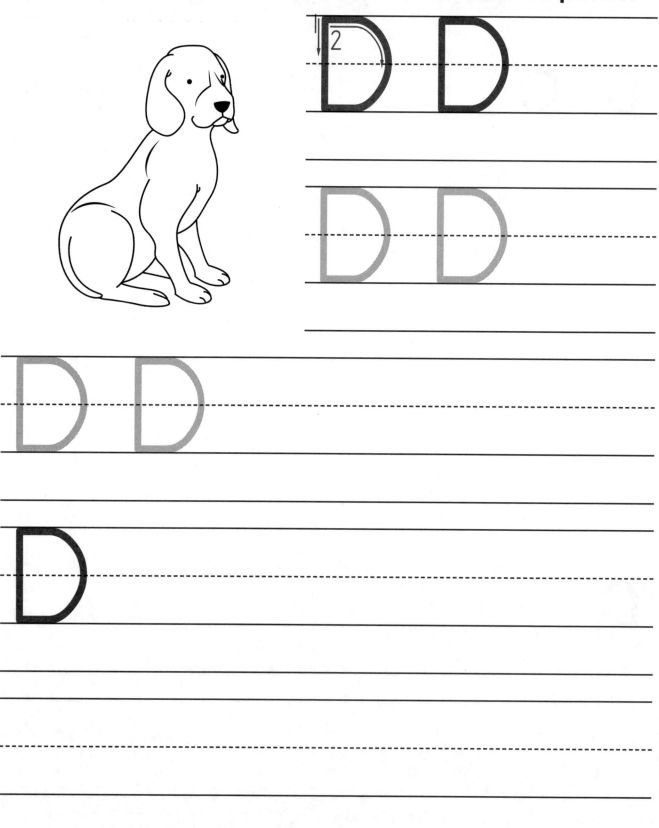

Lowercase Letter D

Trace each letter. Write the letter on the lines. Color the picture.

Uppercase Letter E

Trace each letter. Write the letter on the lines. Color the picture.

Lowercase Letter E

Trace each letter. Write the letter on the lines. Color the picture.

 e

e e

e

Uppercase Letter F

Trace each letter. Write the letter on the lines. Color the picture.

Lowercase Letter F

Trace each letter. Write the letter on the lines. Color the picture.

Uppercase Letter G

Trace each letter. Write the letter on the lines. Color the picture.

Lowercase Letter G

Trace each letter. Write the letter on the lines. Color the picture.

g g

g g

g g

g

Uppercase Letter H

Trace each letter. Write the letter on the lines. Color the picture.

Lowercase Letter H

Trace each letter. Write the letter on the lines. Color the picture.

Uppercase Letter I

Trace each letter. Write the letter on the lines. Color the picture.

Lowercase Letter I

Trace each letter. Write the letter on the lines. Color the picture.

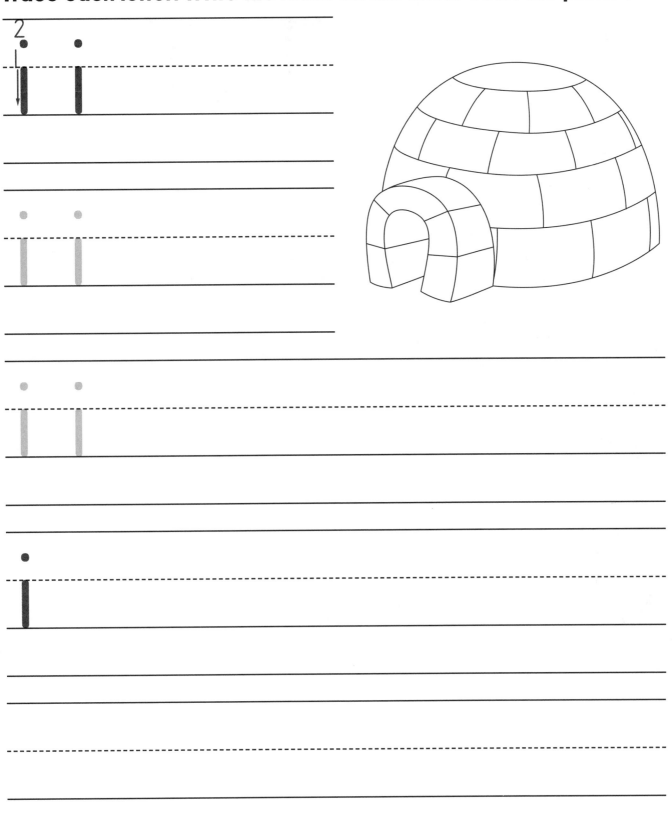

Uppercase Letter J

Trace each letter. Write the letter on the lines. Color the picture.

Lowercase Letter J

Trace each letter. Write the letter on the lines. Color the picture.

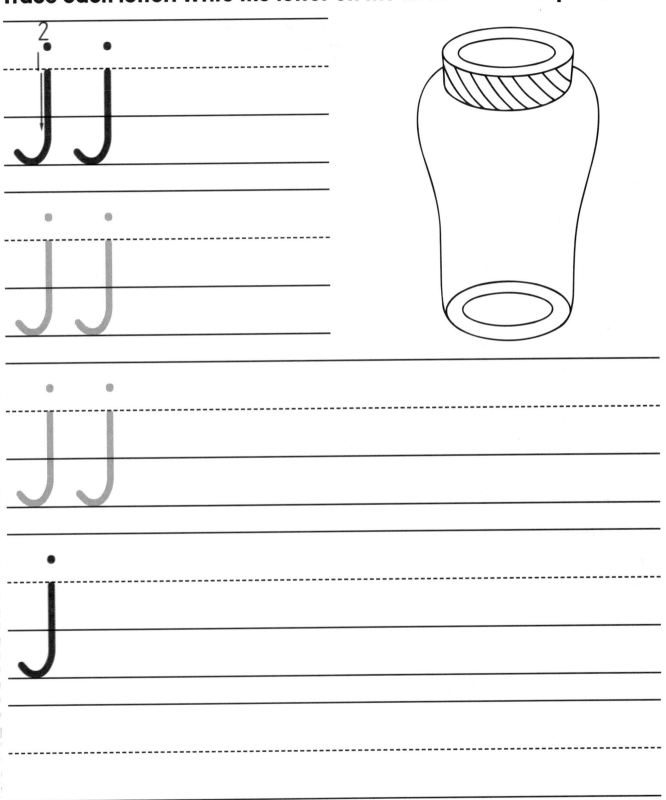

UPPERCASE LETTER K

Trace each letter. Write the letter on the lines. Color the picture.

LOWERCASE LETTER K

Trace each letter. Write the letter on the lines. Color the picture.

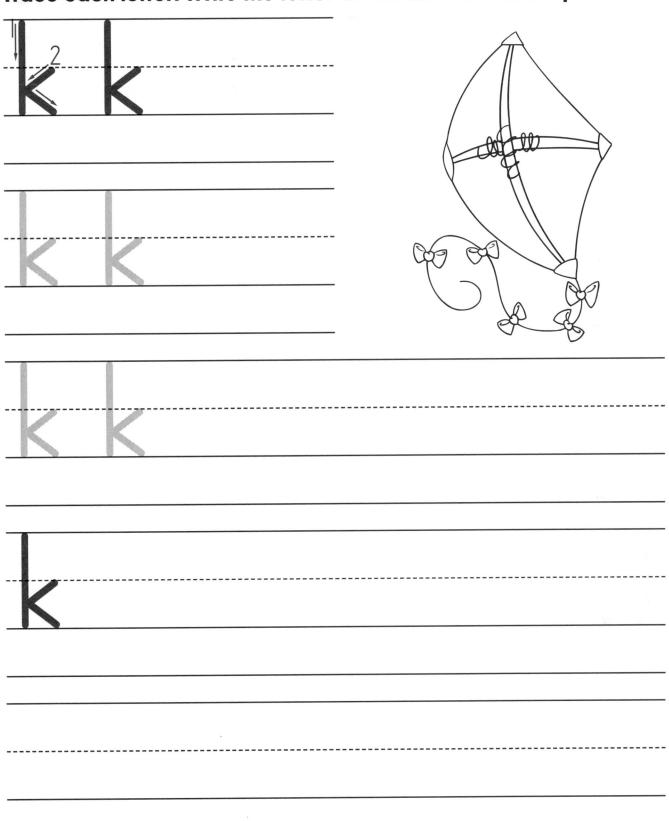

Uppercase Letter L

Trace each letter. Write the letter on the lines. Color the picture.

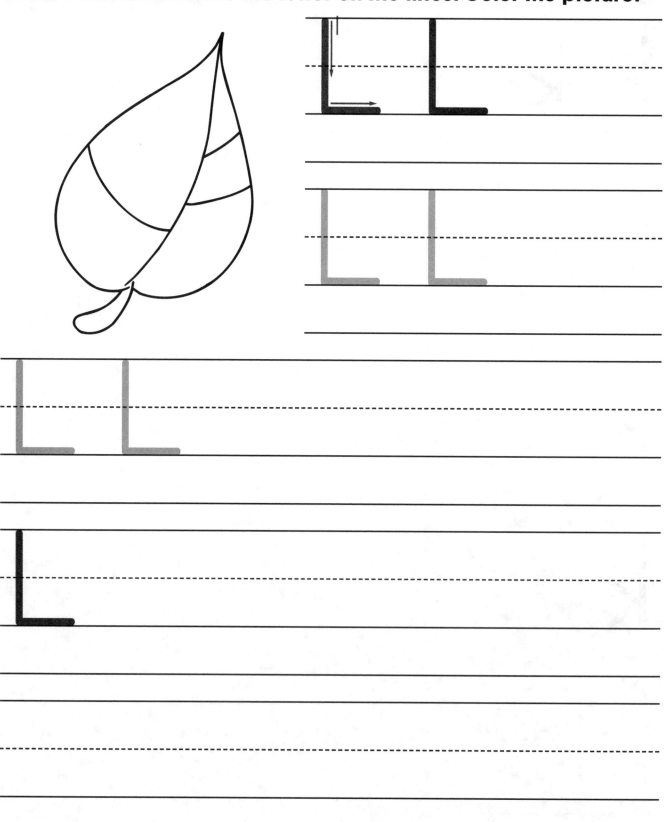

Lowercase Letter L

Trace each letter. Write the letter on the lines. Color the picture.

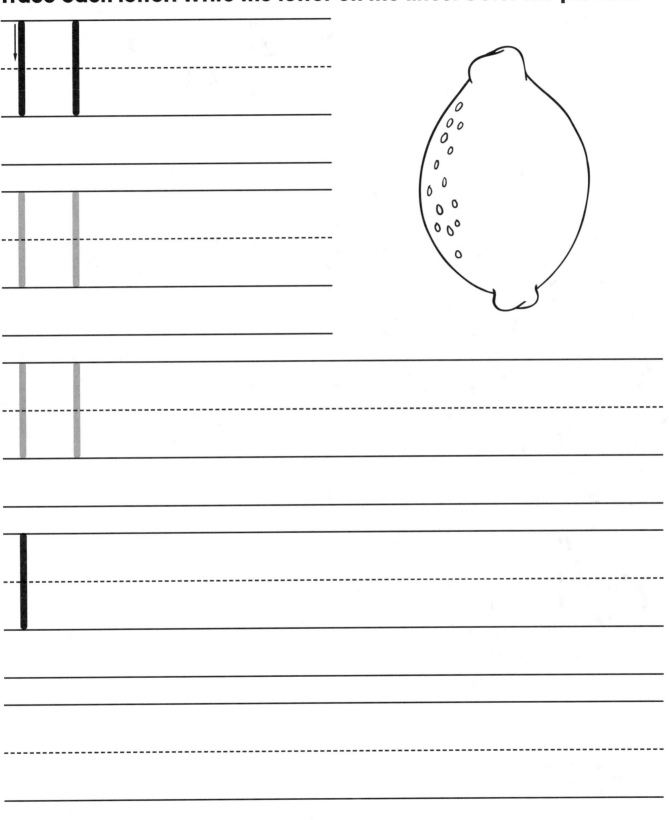

Uppercase Letter M

Trace each letter. Write the letter on the lines. Color the picture.

Lowercase Letter M

Trace each letter. Write the letter on the lines. Color the picture.

m m

m m

m m

m

Uppercase Letter N

Trace each letter. Write the letter on the lines. Color the picture.

Lowercase Letter N

Trace each letter. Write the letter on the lines. Color the picture.

n n

n n

n n

n

Uppercase Letter O

Trace each letter. Write the letter on the lines. Color the picture.

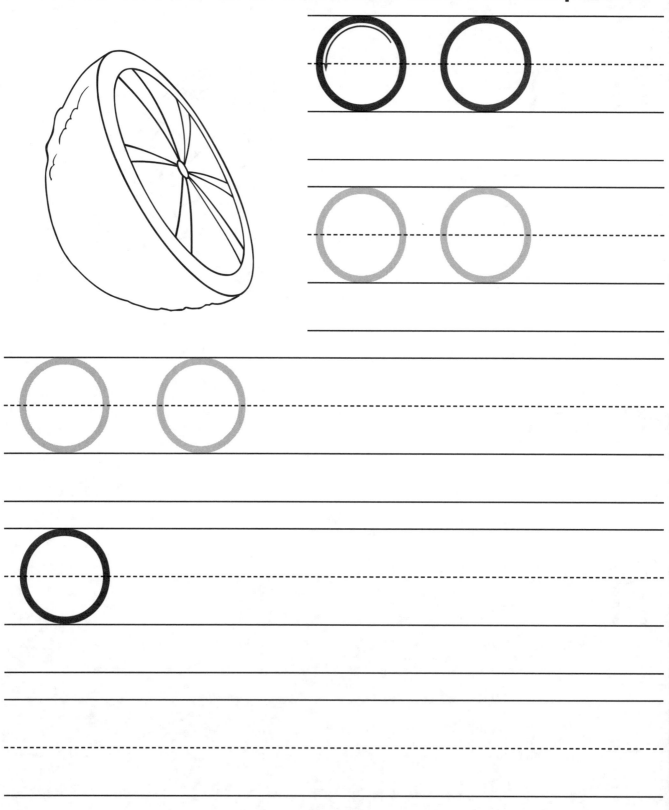

Lowercase Letter o

Trace each letter. Write the letter on the lines. Color the picture.

o o

o o

o o

o

Uppercase Letter P

Trace each letter. Write the letter on the lines. Color the picture.

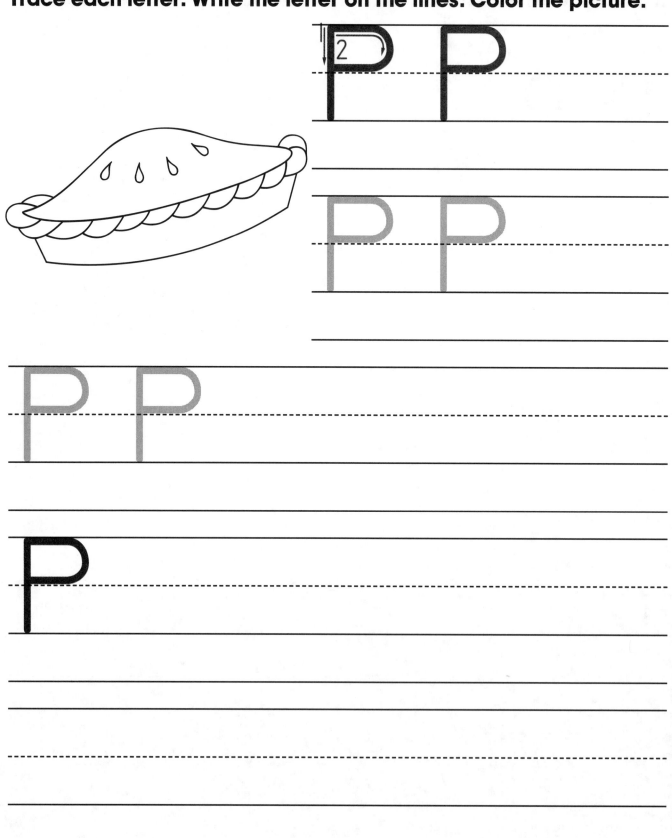

Lowercase Letter P

Trace each letter. Write the letter on the lines. Color the picture.

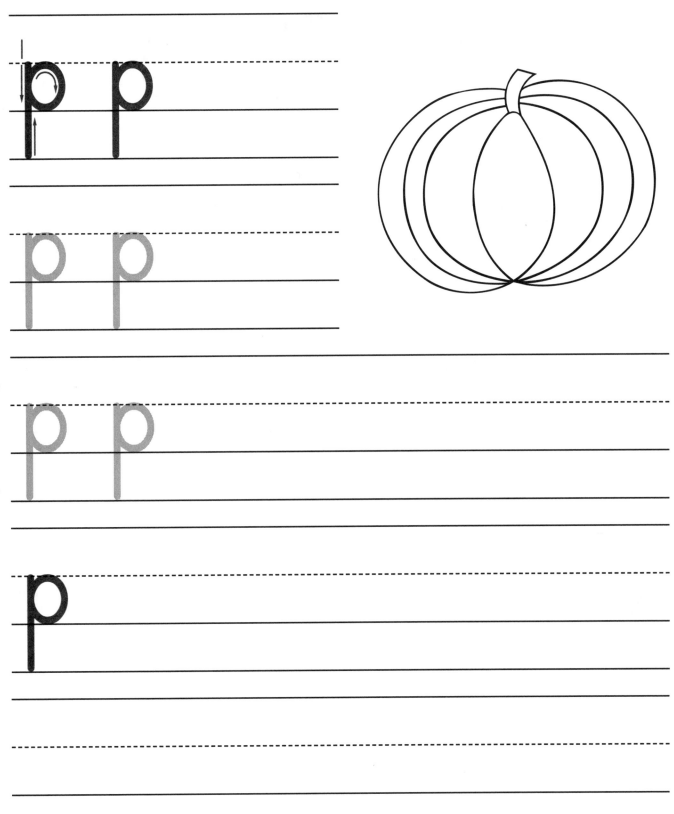

Uppercase Letter Q

Trace each letter. Write the letter on the lines. Color the picture.

Lowercase Letter Q

Trace each letter. Write the letter on the lines. Color the picture.

Uppercase Letter R

Trace each letter. Write the letter on the lines. Color the picture.

Lowercase Letter R

Trace each letter. Write the letter on the lines. Color the picture.

r r

r r

r r

r

Uppercase Letter S

Trace each letter. Write the letter on the lines. Color the picture.

Lowercase Letter S

Trace each letter. Write the letter on the lines. Color the picture.

Uppercase Letter T

Trace each letter. Write the letter on the lines. Color the picture.

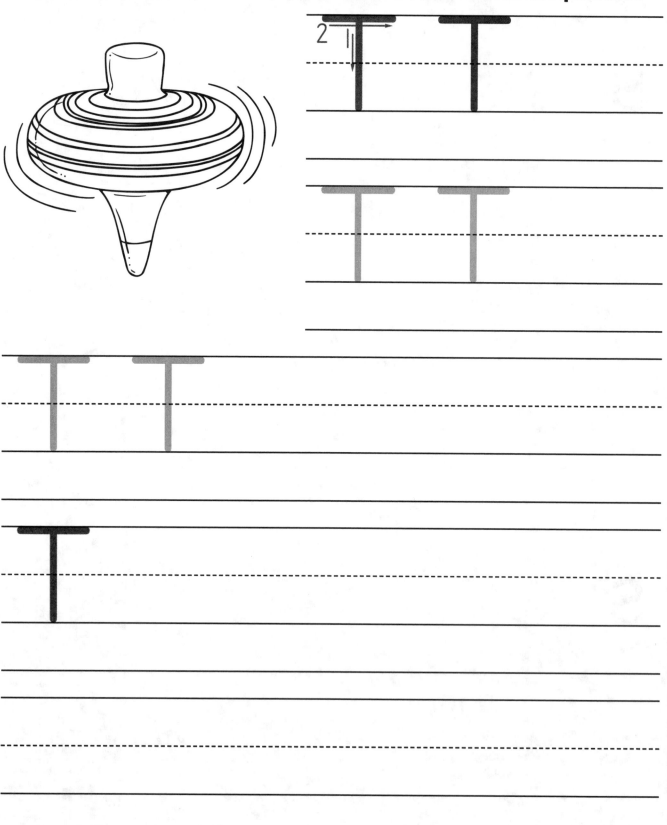

Lowercase Letter T

Trace each letter. Write the letter on the lines. Color the picture.

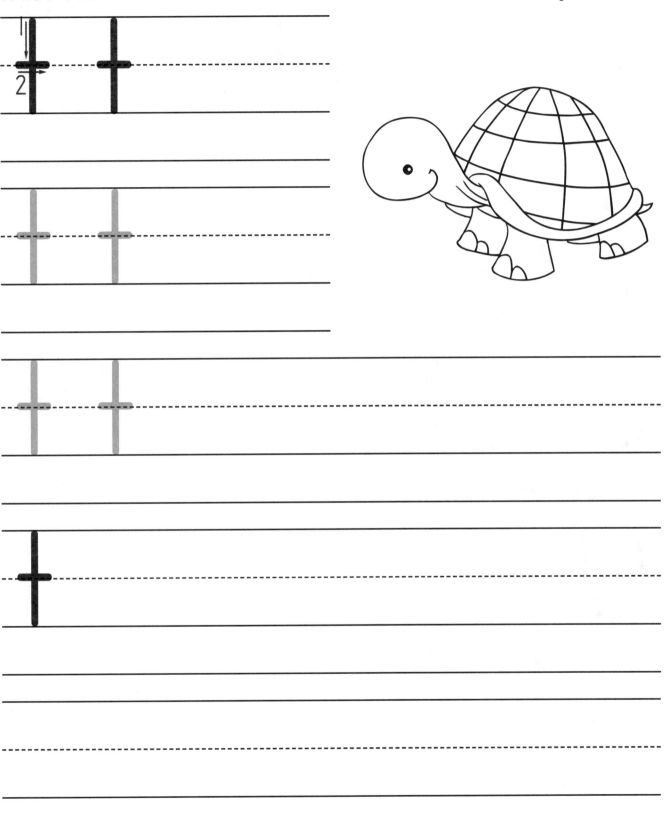

Uppercase Letter U

Trace each letter. Write the letter on the lines. Color the picture.

Lowercase Letter U

Trace each letter. Write the letter on the lines. Color the picture.

u u

u u

u u

u

Uppercase Letter V

Trace each letter. Write the letter on the lines. Color the picture.

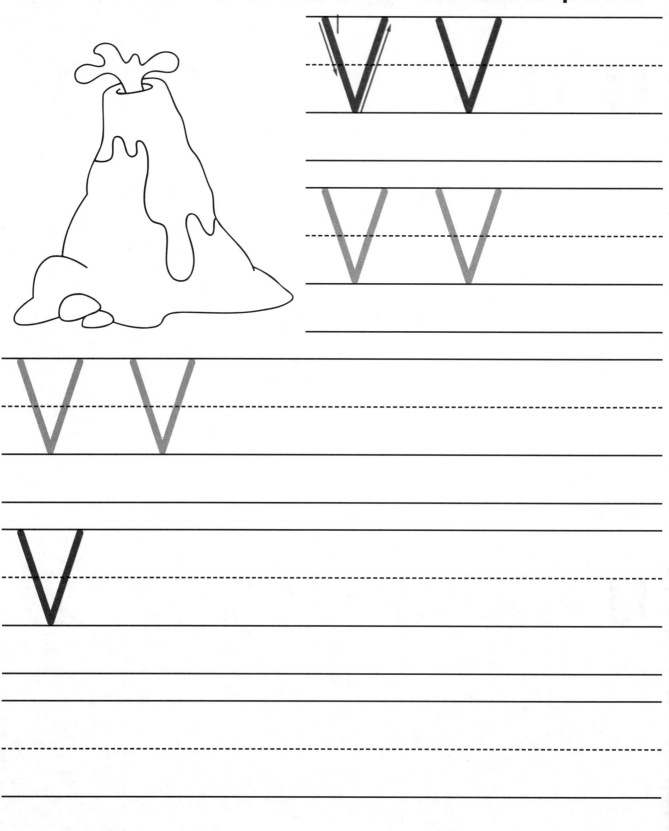

Lowercase Letter V

Trace each letter. Write the letter on the lines. Color the picture.

V V

v v

v v

v

Uppercase Letter W

Trace each letter. Write the letter on the lines. Color the picture.

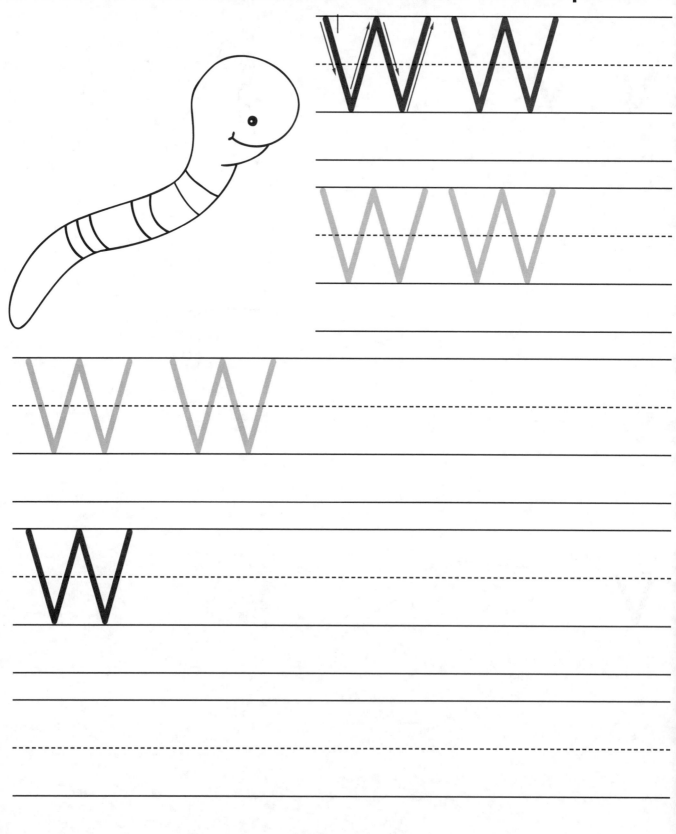

Lowercase Letter W

Trace each letter. Write the letter on the lines. Color the picture.

w w w

w w

w w

w

Uppercase Letter X

Trace each letter. Write the letter on the lines. Color the picture.

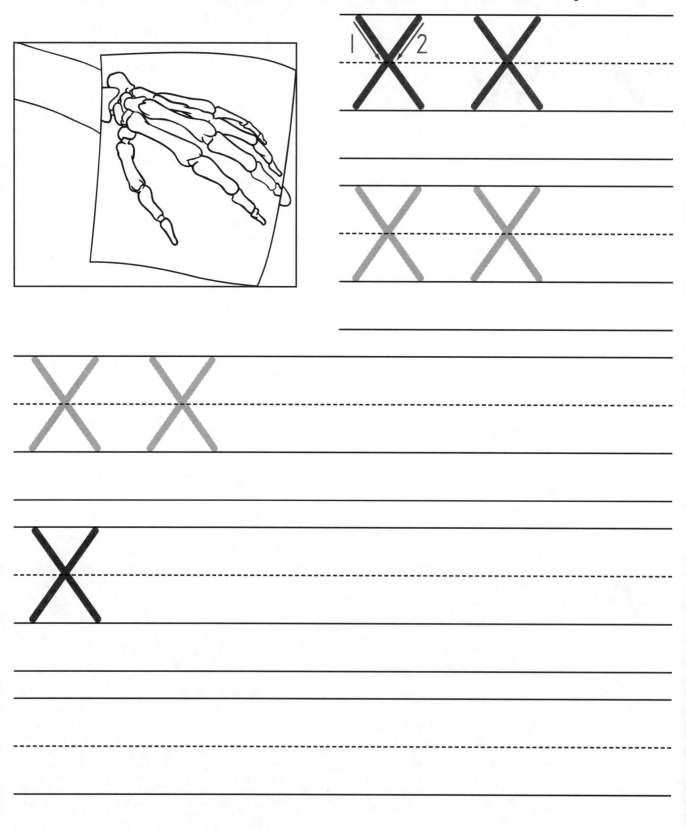

Lowercase Letter X

Trace each letter. Write the letter on the lines. Color the picture.

1 2
X X

X X

X X

X

Uppercase Letter Y

Trace each letter. Write the letter on the lines. Color the picture.

Lowercase Letter y

Trace each letter. Write the letter on the lines. Color the picture.

y y y

y y

y y

y

Uppercase Letter Z

Trace each letter. Write the letter on the lines. Color the picture.

Lowercase Letter Z

Trace each letter. Write the letter on the lines. Color the picture.

z z

z z

z z

z

Matching Letters

Draw a line from each uppercase letter to its matching lowercase letter.

M

H

W

V

N

U

u

v

n

m

h

w

Matching Letters

Draw a line from each uppercase letter to its matching lowercase letter.

B

P

Q

G

D

R

q

g

p

r

b

d

Matching Letters

Draw a line from each uppercase letter to its matching lowercase letter.

Y

A

O

Z

C

E

S

z

c

a

s

e

y

o

Matching Letters

Draw a line from each uppercase letter to its matching lowercase letter.

J

L

X

F

K

I

T

x

j

i

k

t

f

l

Matching Letters

Draw a line from each uppercase letter to its matching lowercase letter.

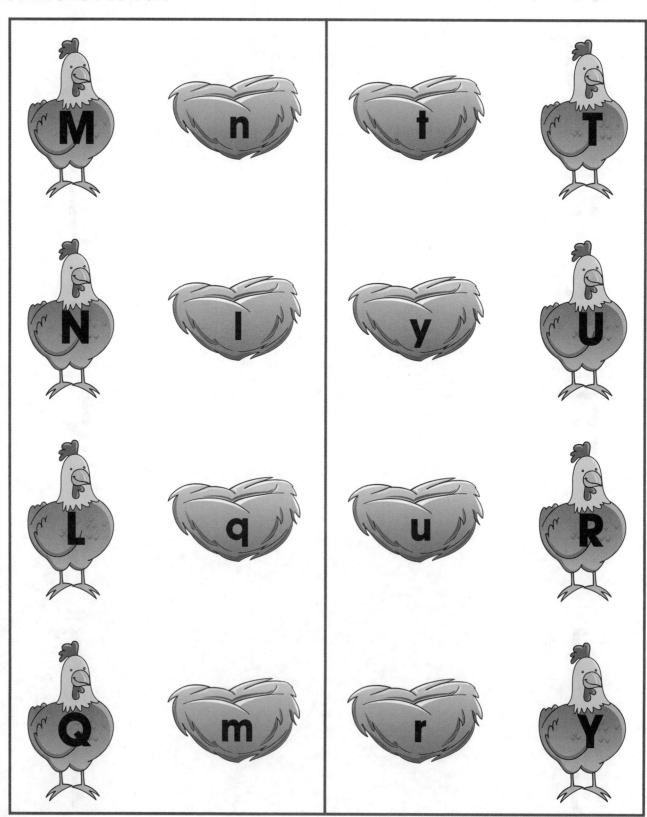

Missing Letters

Write each missing uppercase or lowercase letter.

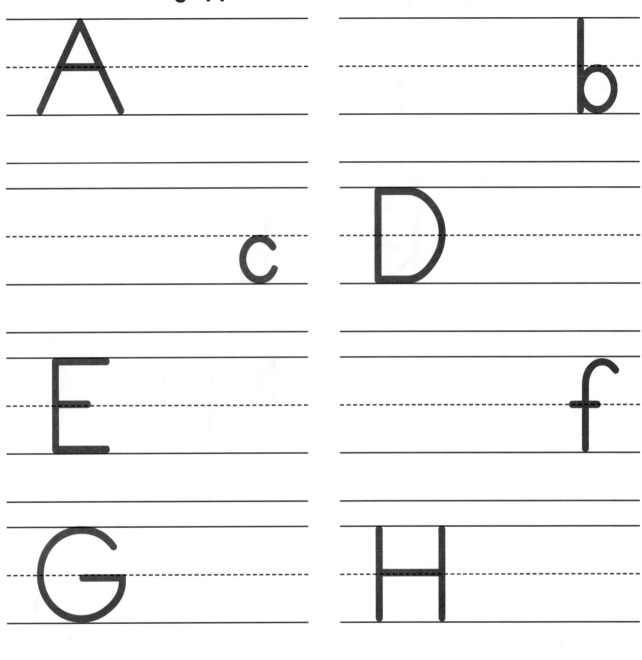

A   b

c   D

E   f

G   H

Missing Letters

Write each missing uppercase or lowercase letter.

i   j

k   L

m   N

O   p

Missing Letters

Write each missing uppercase or lowercase letter.

q   R

S   t

U   v

W   x

y   Z

Letter Review

Write the matching lowercase letter next to each uppercase letter. Color the pictures.

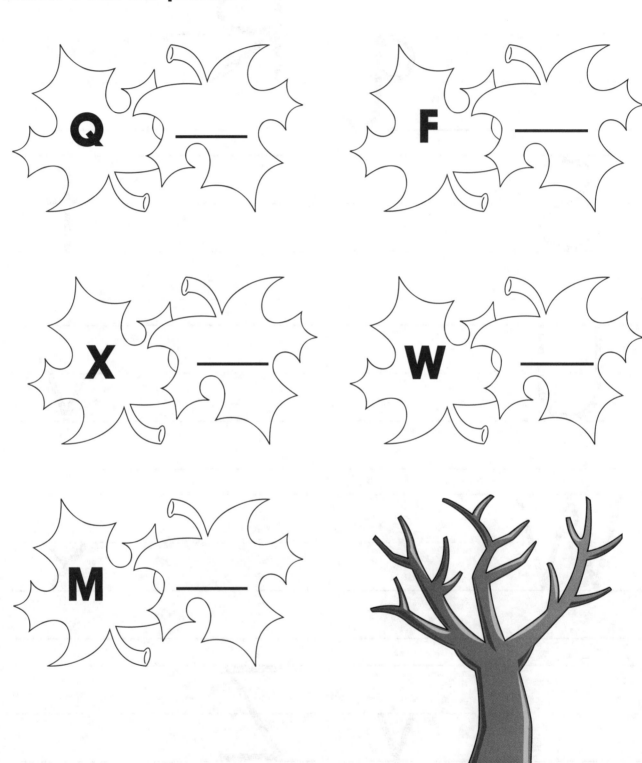

Q ___

F ___

X ___

W ___

M ___

Letter Review

Write the matching lowercase letter next to each uppercase letter.

Letter Review

Write the matching uppercase letter next to each lowercase letter.

Letter Review

Write the matching uppercase letter next to each lowercase letter. Color the flowers.

Beginning Sounds

Draw a line from each picture to the letter that makes its beginning sound.

D

L

P

R

Beginning Sounds

Draw a line from each picture to the letter that makes its beginning sound.

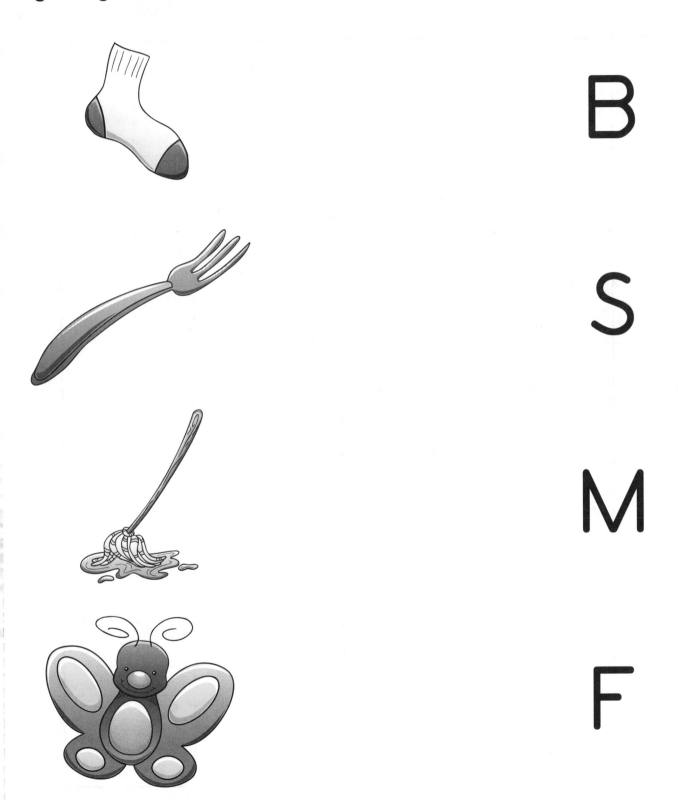

B

S

M

F

Hidden Picture

Use the code to color the spaces and find the hidden picture.

p = **purple**   g = **green**   y = yellow

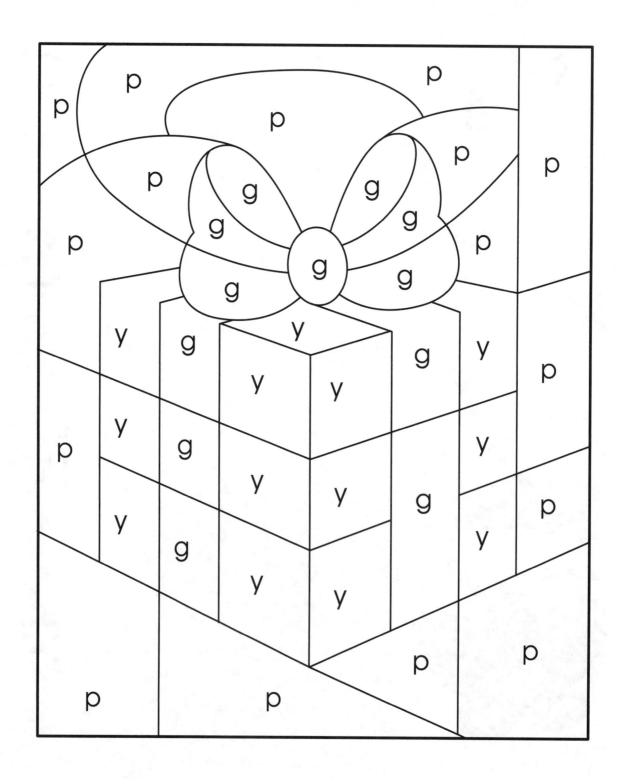

Hidden Picture

Use the code to color the spaces and find the hidden picture.

b = **brown**   g = **green**   y = **yellow**   p = **pink**

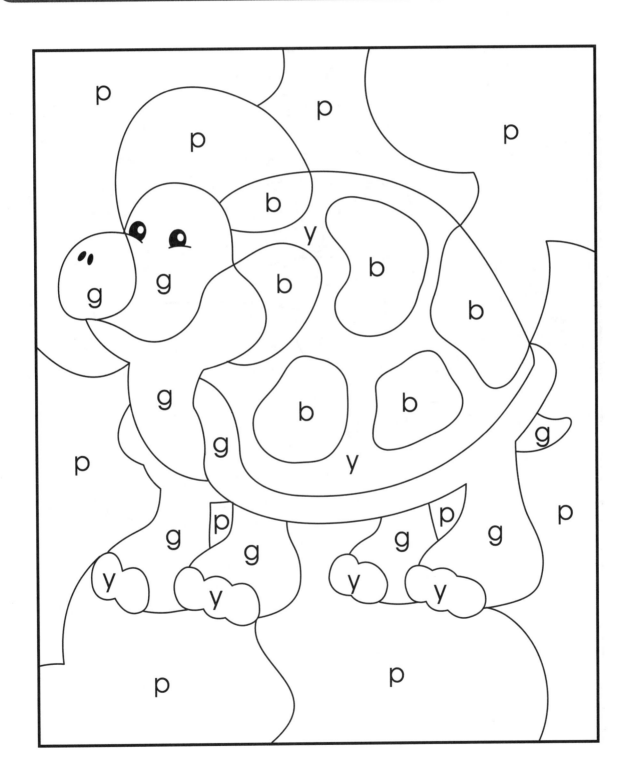

Hidden Picture

Use the code to color the spaces and find the hidden picture.

r = **red**   y = yellow   b = **blue**   g = **green**

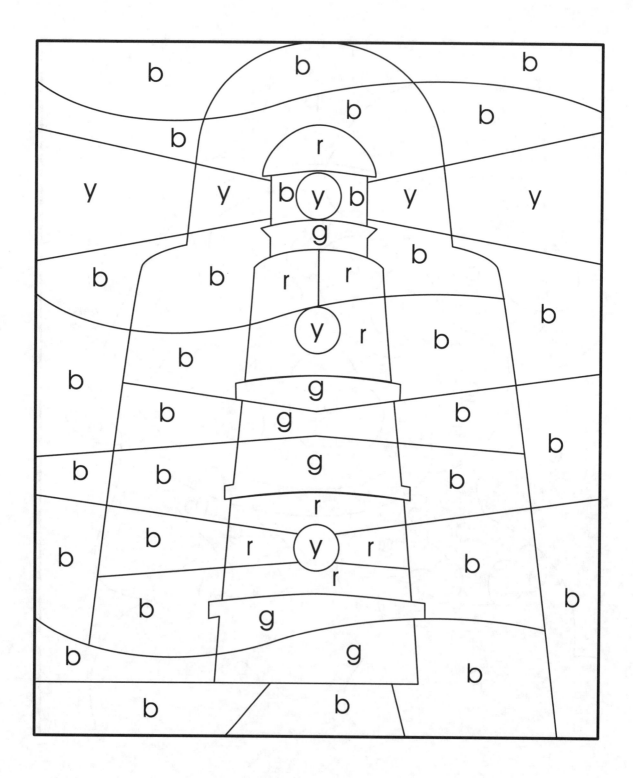

Hidden Picture

Use the code to color the spaces and find the hidden picture.

y = yellow   g = green   r = red   b = blue

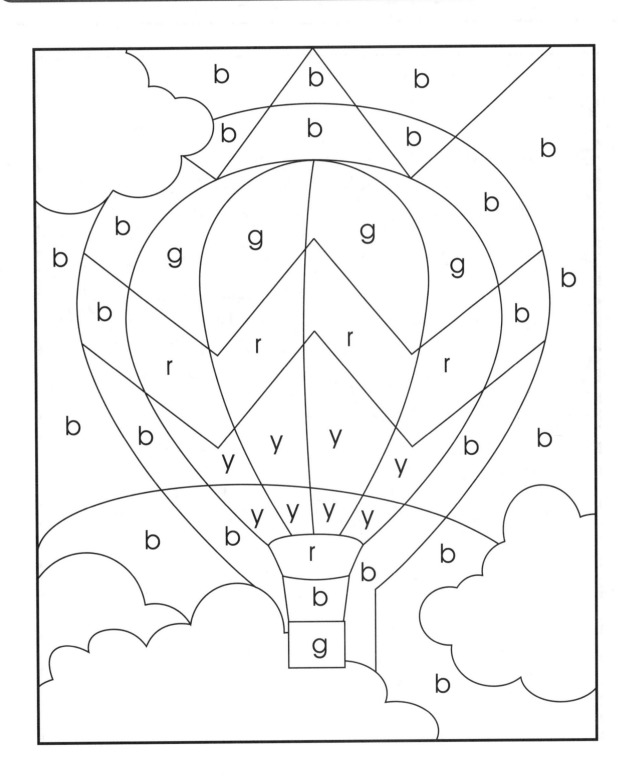

Hidden Picture

Use the code to color the spaces and find the hidden picture.

y = yellow	p = pink	o = orange
g = green	b = blue	

Dot-to-Dot Uppercase A-F

Connect the dots from A to F. Start at the ★. Color the picture.

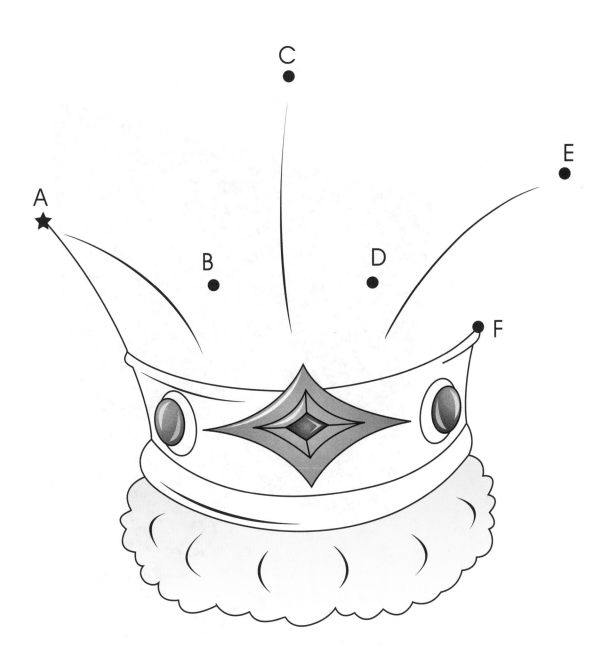

Dot-to-Dot Uppercase A-F

Connect the dots from A to F. Start at the ★. Color the picture.

Dot-to-Dot Uppercase A-F

Connect the dots from A to F. Start at the ★. Color the picture.

Dot-to-Dot Uppercase A-F

Connect the dots from A to F. Start at the ★. Color the picture.

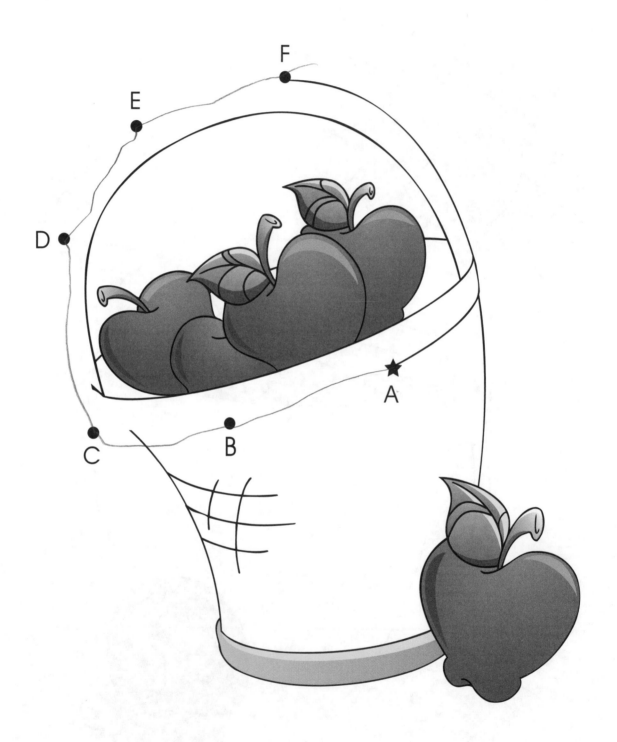

Dot-to-Dot Uppercase A-F

Connect the dots from A to F. Start at the ★. Color the picture.

Dot-to-Dot Uppercase A–K

Connect the dots from A to K. Start at the ★. Color the picture.

A

B

C

D

E

F

G

H

I

J

K

Dot-to-dot Uppercase A-K

Connect the dots from A to K. Start at the ★. Color the picture.

Dot-to-Dot Uppercase A-K

Connect the dots from A to K. Start at the ★. Color the picture.

Dot-to-Dot Uppercase A-K

Connect the dots from A to K. Start at the ★. Color the picture.

Dot-to-Dot Uppercase A-K

Connect the dots from A to K. Start at the ★. Color the picture.

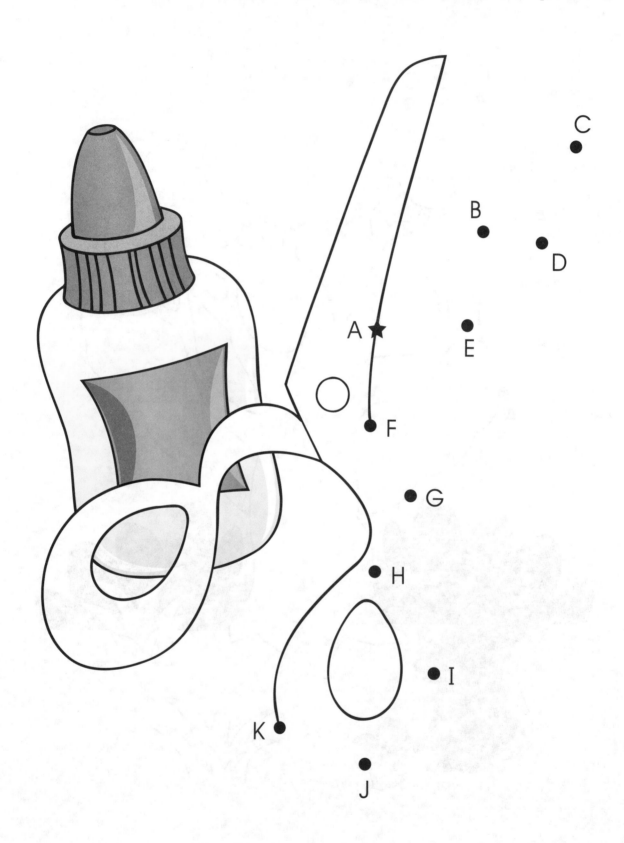

Dot-to-Dot Uppercase A-K

Connect the dots from A to K. Start at the ★. Color the picture.

Dot-to-Dot Uppercase A-P

Connect the dots from A to P. Start at the ★. Color the picture.

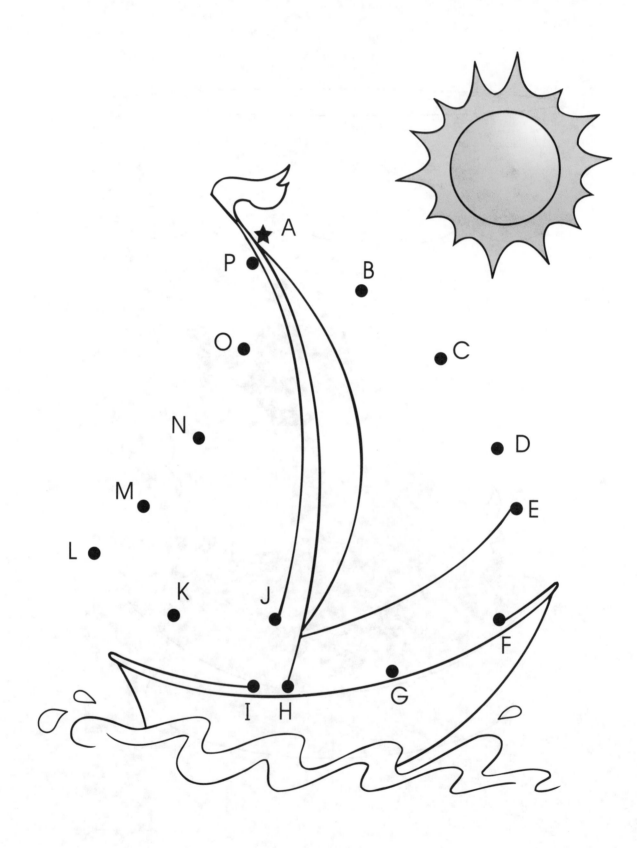

Dot-to-Dot Uppercase A-P

Connect the dots from A to P. Start at the ★. Color the picture.

Dot-to-Dot Uppercase A-P

Connect the dots from A to P. Start at the ★. Color the picture.

Dot-to-Dot Uppercase A-P

Connect the dots from A to P. Start at the ★. Color the picture.

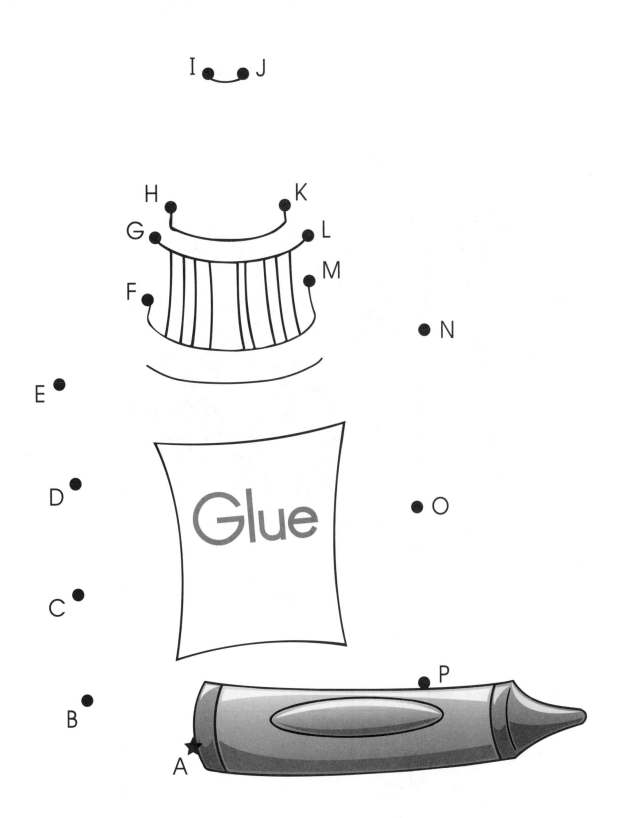

Dot-to-Dot Uppercase A-P

Connect the dots from A to P. Start at the ★. Color the picture.

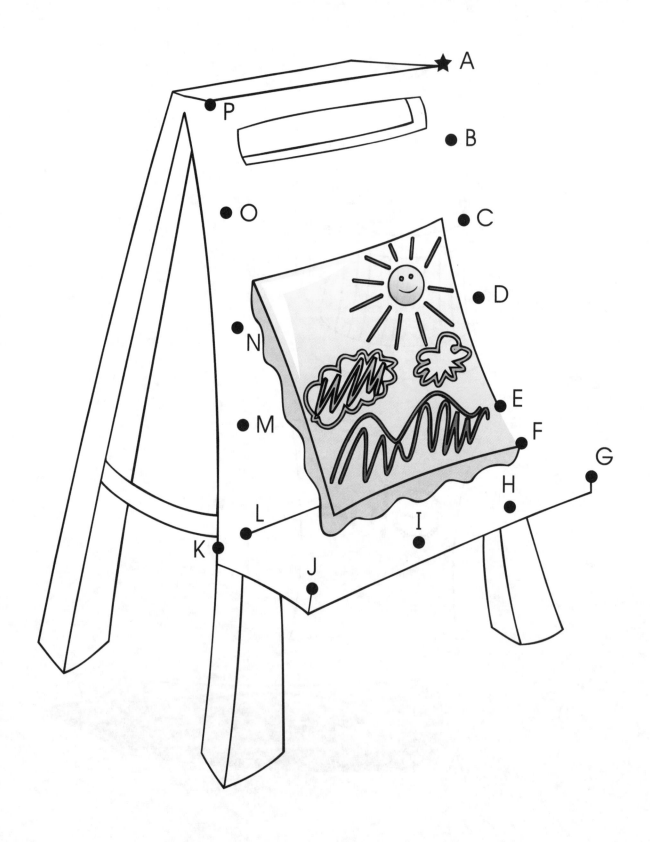

Dot-to-Dot Uppercase A-P

Connect the dots from A to P. Start at the ★. Color the picture.

Dot-to-Dot Uppercase A-U

Connect the dots from A to U. Start at the ★. Color the picture.

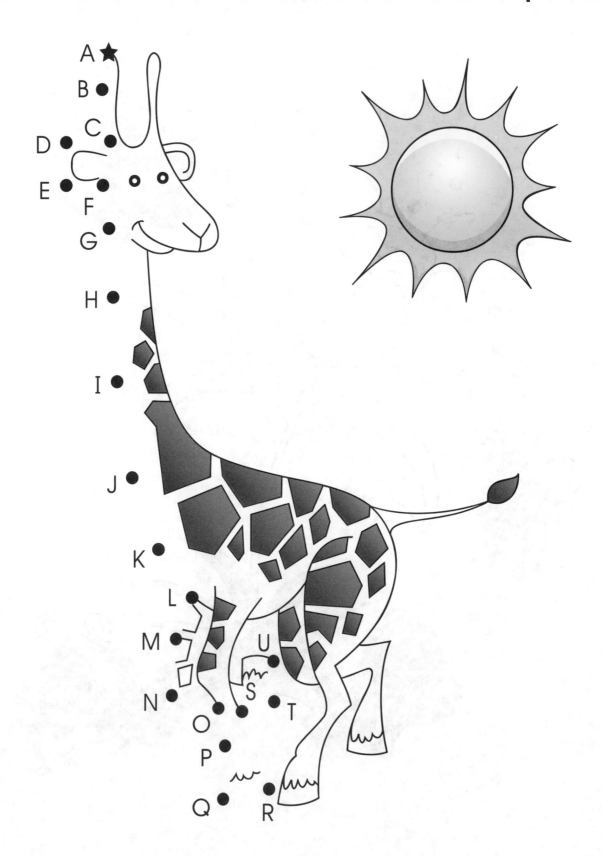

Dot-to-Dot Uppercase A-U

Connect the dots from A to U. Start at the ★. Color the picture.

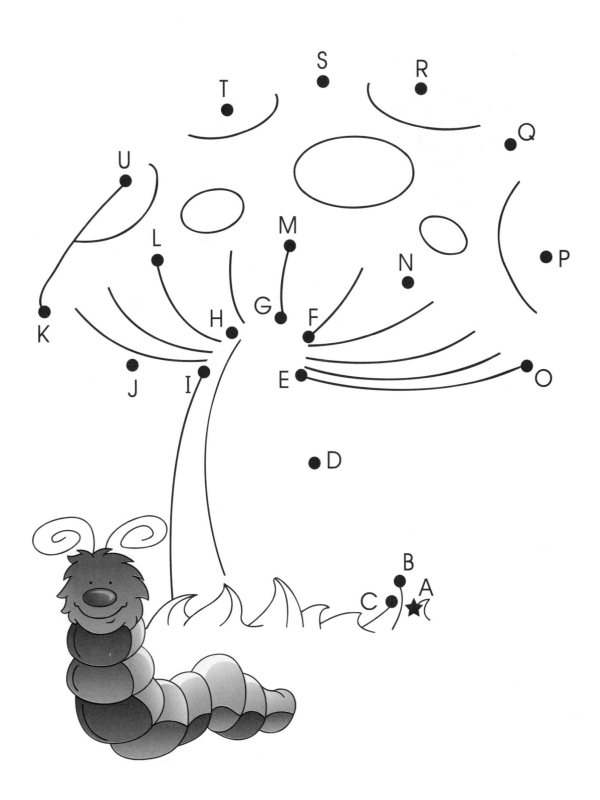

Dot-to-Dot Uppercase A–U

Connect the dots from A to U. Start at the ★. Color the picture.

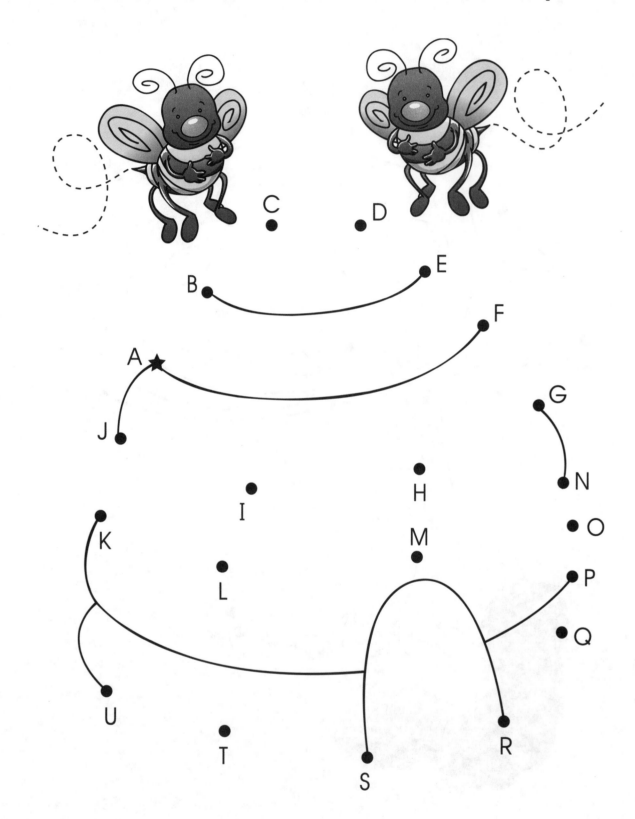

Dot-to-Dot Uppercase A-U

Connect the dots from A to U. Start at the ★. Color the picture.

Dot-to-Dot Uppercase A–U

Connect the dots from A to U. Start at the ★. Color the picture.

Dot-to-Dot Uppercase A-Z

Connect the dots from A to Z. Start at the ★. Color the picture.

Dot-to-Dot Uppercase A-Z

Connect the dots from A to Z. Start at the ★. Color the picture.

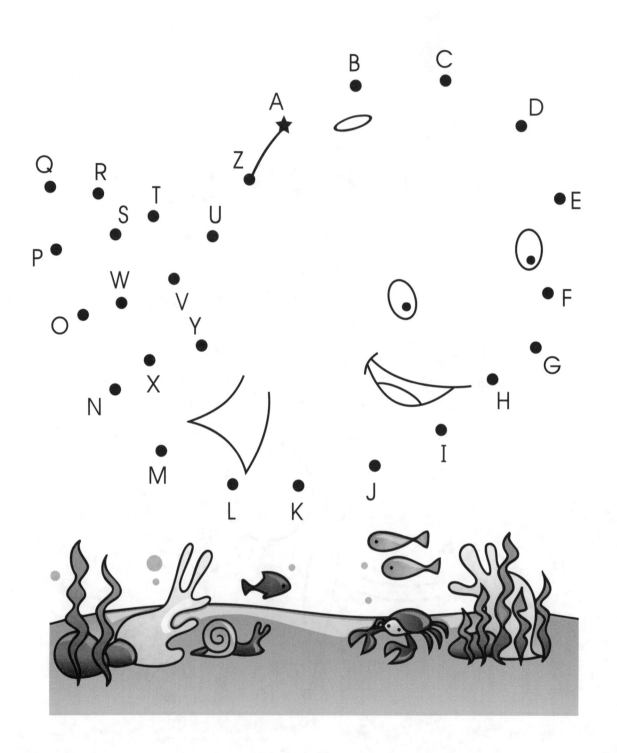

Dot-to-Dot Uppercase A-Z

Connect the dots from A to Z. Start at the ★. Color the picture.

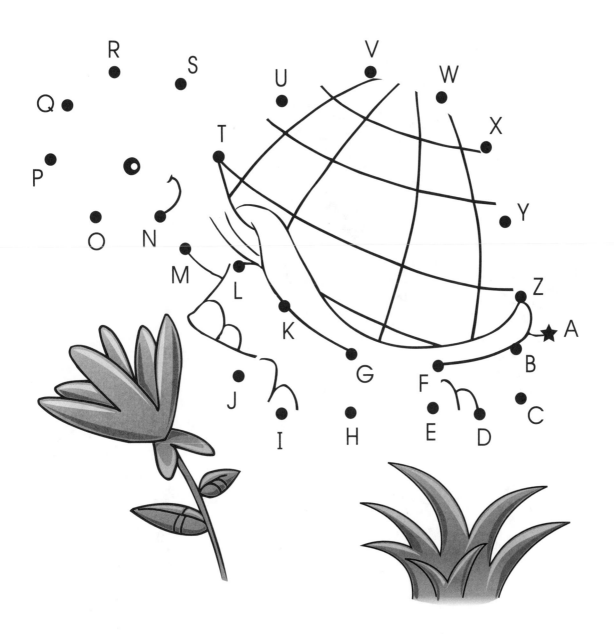

Dot-to-Dot Uppercase A-Z

Connect the dots from A to Z. Start at the ★. Color the picture.

Dot-to-Dot Lowercase A-K

Connect the dots from a to k. Start at the ★. Color the picture.

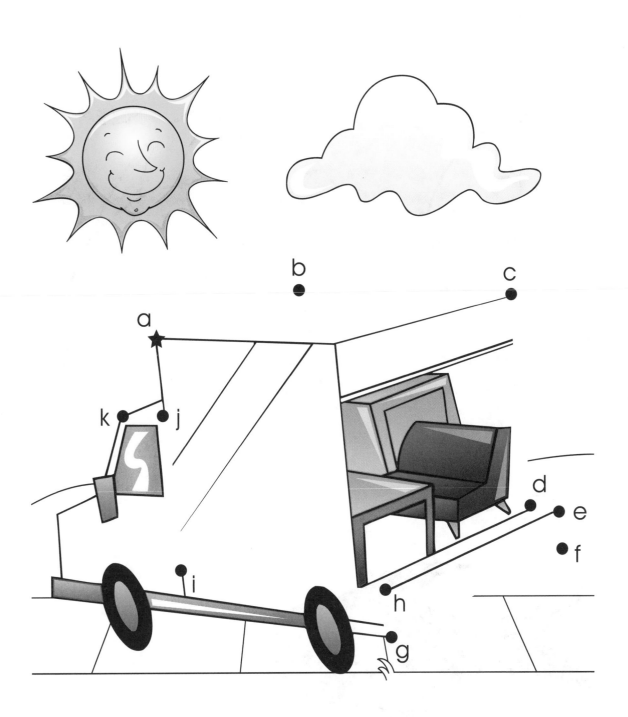

Dot-to-Dot Lowercase A-K

Connect the dots from a to k. Start at the ★. Color the picture.

Dot-to-Dot Lowercase A-K

Connect the dots from a to p. Start at the ★. Color the picture.

Dot-to-Dot Lowercase A-Z

Connect the dots from a to z. Start at the ★. Color the picture.

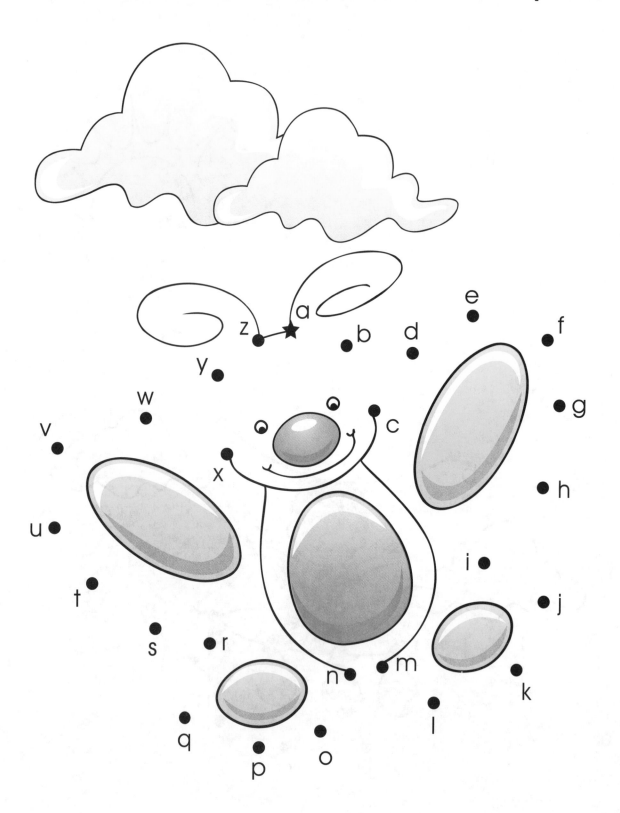

Dot-to-Dot Lowercase A-Z

Connect the dots from a to z. Start at the ★. Color the picture.

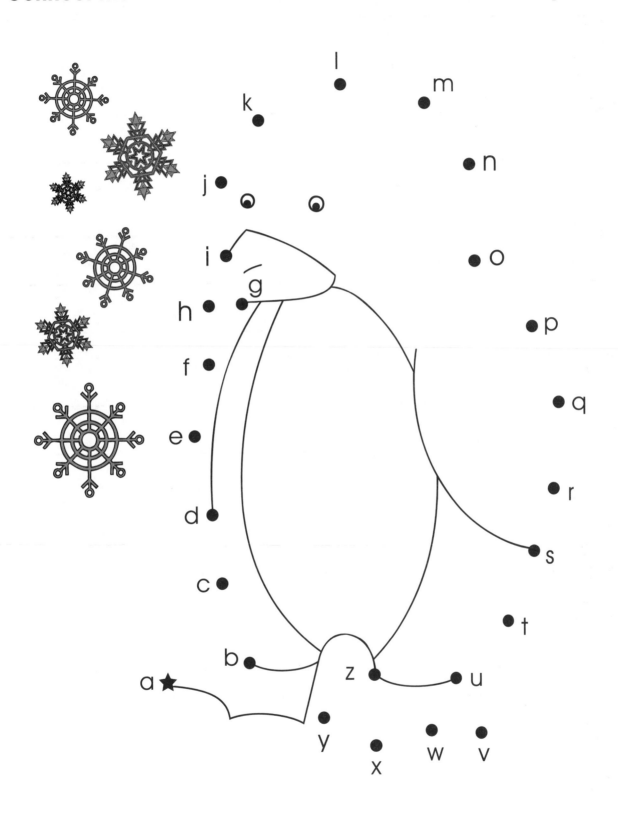

Numbers 0-4

Trace each number. Write each number on the line.

0 0

1 1

2 2

3 3

4 4

Numbers 5-9

Trace each number. Write each number on the line.

5 5 _____

6 6 _____

7 7 _____

8 8 _____

9 9 _____

Counting 0 to 5

Draw a line from each number to the box with the matching set.

0

1

2

3

4

5

Counting 6 to 10

Draw a line from each number to the box with the matching set.

6

7

8

9

10

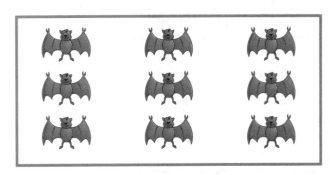

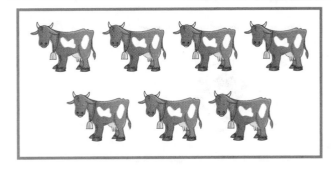

Matching Sets

Draw a line to connect each pair of boxes that have the same number of pictures.

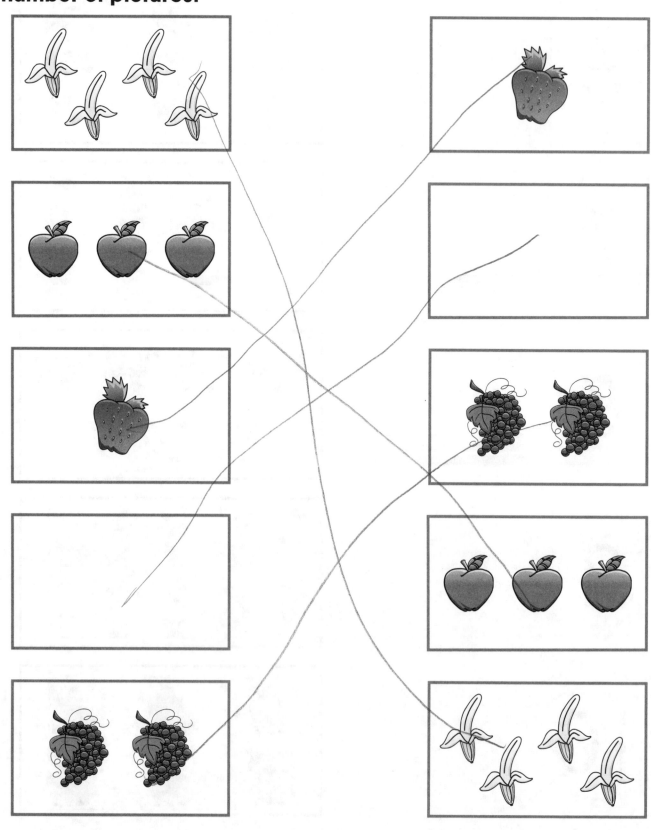

Matching Sets

Draw a line to connect each pair of boxes that have the same number of pictures.

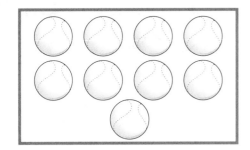

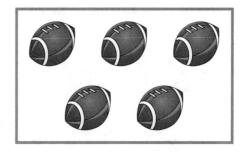

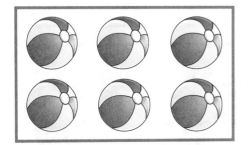

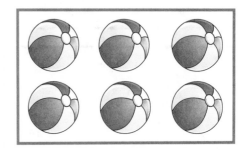

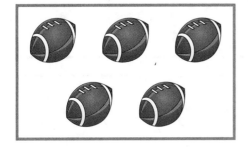

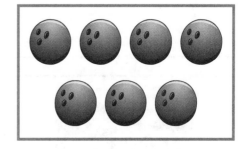

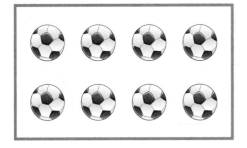

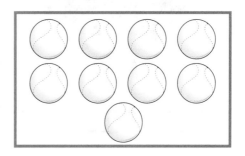

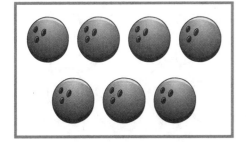

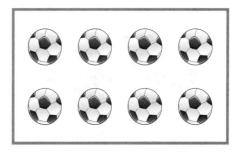

161

Matching Sets

Draw a line to connect each pair of boxes that have the same number of pictures.

Matching Sets

Color and cut out the shapes. Paste each shape on the flower with the matching number. Color the picture.

Counting 0 to 5

Circle the number of pictures in each box to match each number.

0	
1	
2	
3	
4	
5	

Counting 6 to 10

Circle the number of pictures in each box to match each number.

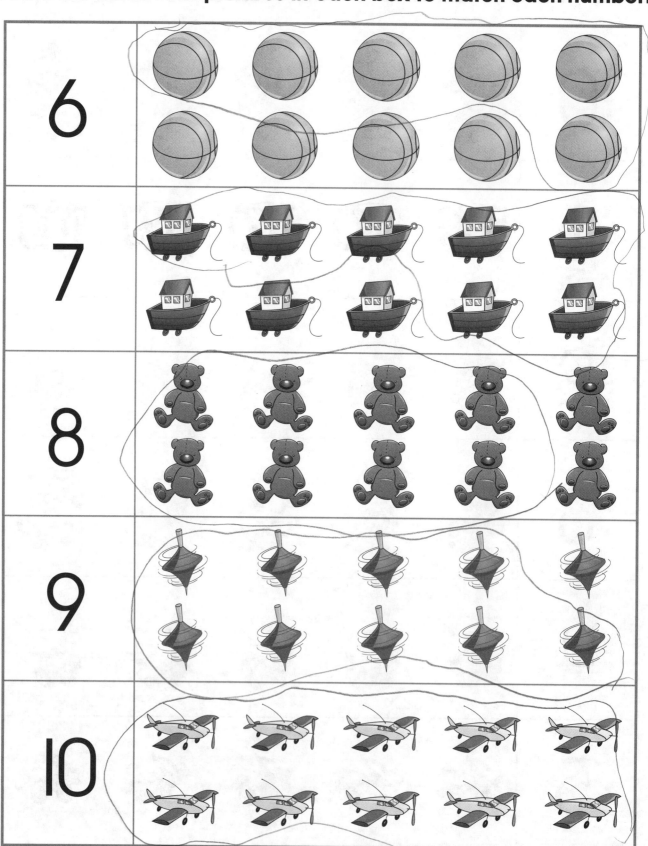

How Many?

Count the number of objects in each row. Write the number of objects on the line.

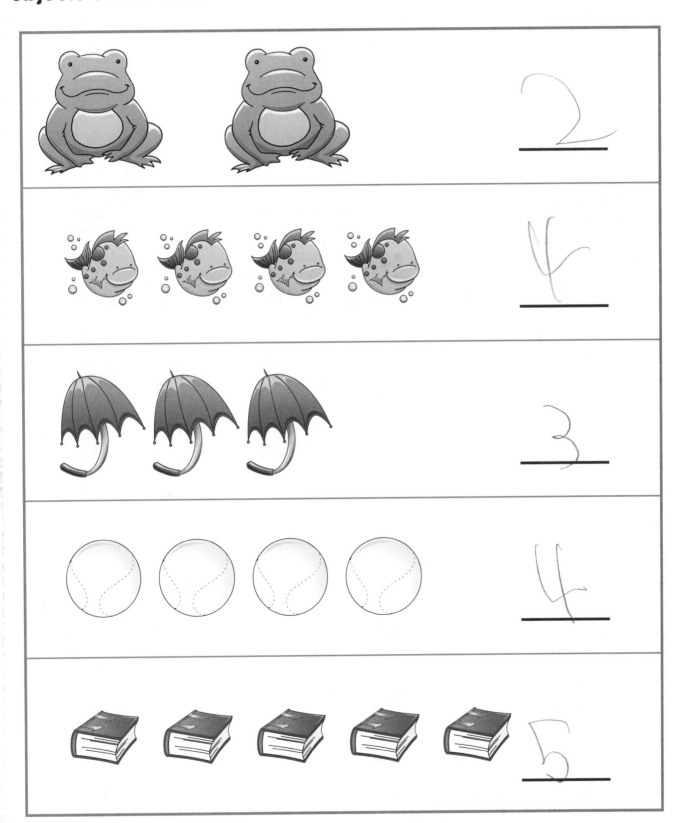

2

4

3

4

5

Gum Balls 0-5

Look at the number below each gum ball machine. Draw the matching number of gum balls in each machine.

3

2

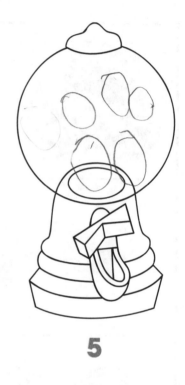

5

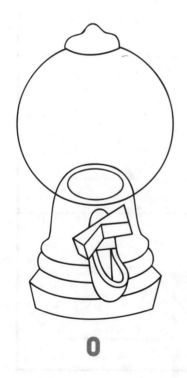

0

1

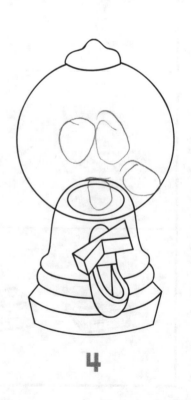

4

Gum Balls 6-10

Look at the number below each gum ball machine. Draw the matching number of gum balls in each machine.

7

8

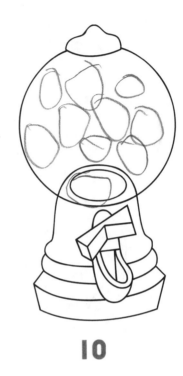

10

9

6

Up to Ten

Number the shapes in order from 0 to 10 to help the astronaut reach the moon. Color the picture.

Up to Ten

Number the lily pads in order from 0 to 10 to help the frog find his friend. Color the picture.

Number Word Match

Draw a line from each numeral to its number word.

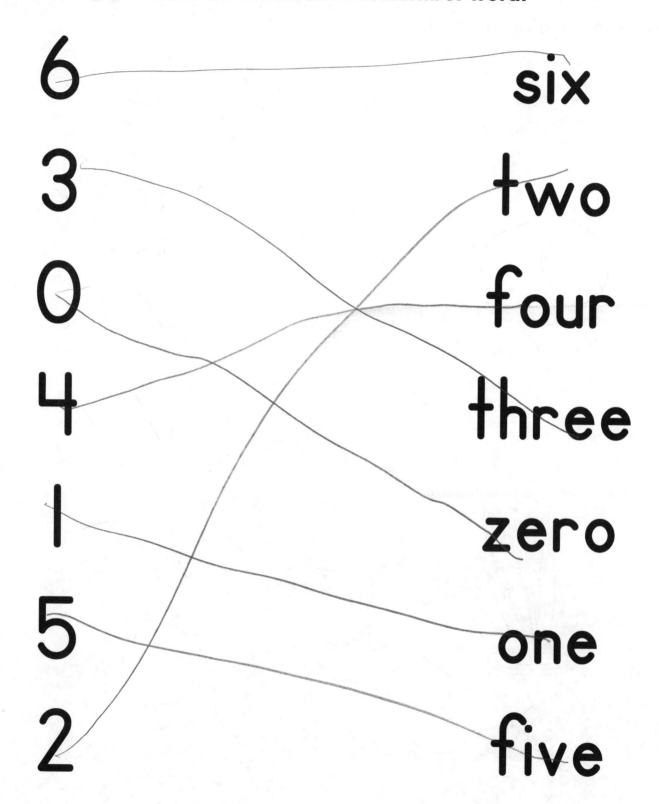

6   six

3   two

0   four

4   three

1   zero

5   one

2   five

Number Word Match

Draw a line from each numeral to its number word.

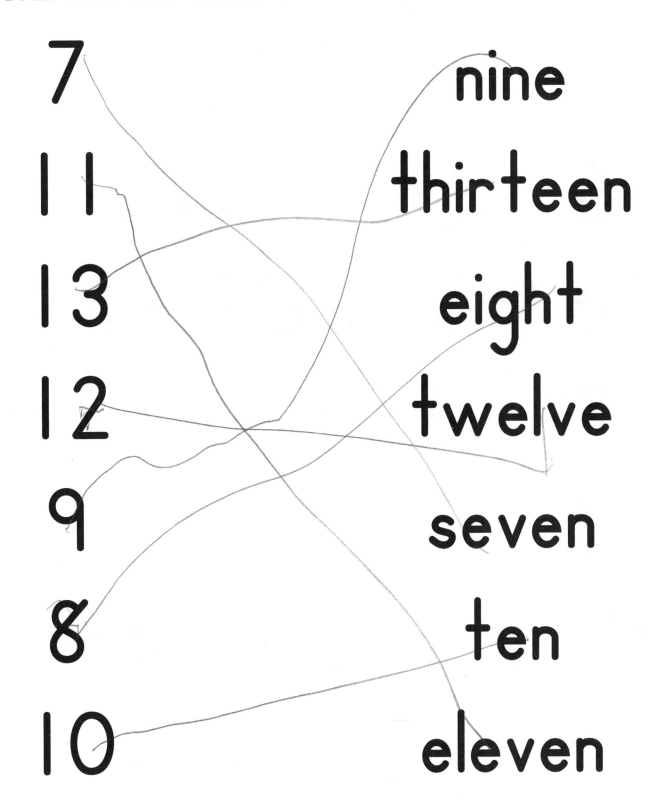

Number Word Match

Draw a line from each numeral to its number word.

19	fifteen
16	nineteen
14	eighteen
17	twenty
18	sixteen
15	fourteen
20	seventeen

Number Riddle

Look at each number. Find the set in the secret code that has the same number of dots. Write the letter on the line above the matching number.

What did one wall say to the other wall?

8 5 5 9   4 6 0

3 9   9 I 5

7 6 2 I0 5 2 !

Secret Code

:: = Y   :: = E   .. = R   :: :: = N

... = A   ::. = C   ::: = O   = U

::: = T   :::: = M   . = H

Hidden Objects

Help the teacher find 4 apples 🍎. Circle all of the apples 🍎. Color the picture.

Hidden Objects

Help the catcher find 4 bananas . Circle all of the bananas. Color the picture.

Hidden Objects

Help the birds find 3 pencils . Circle all of the pencils . Color the picture.

Hidden Objects

Help the girl find 5 pieces of cheese . Circle all of the pieces of cheese. Color the picture.

Hidden Objects

Help the friends find 6 crayons . Circle all of the crayons. Color the picture.

Hidden Objects

Circle the 3 hidden objects. Color the picture.

Hidden Objects

Circle the 4 hidden objects. Color the picture.

Hidden Objects

Circle the 4 hidden objects. Color the picture.

Hidden Objects

Circle the 4 hidden objects. Color the picture.

Hidden Objects

Circle the **6** hidden objects. Color the picture.

Hidden Objects

Circle the 6 hidden objects. Color the picture.

Hidden Picture

Use the code to color the spaces and find the hidden picture.

1 = **purple**　　　　2 = yellow

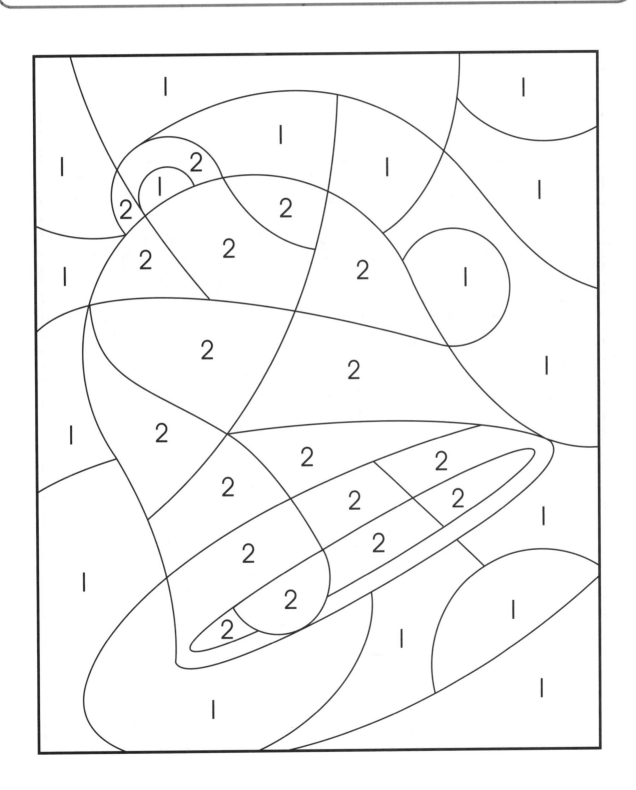

Hidden Picture

Use the code to color the spaces and find the hidden picture.

3 = **blue**	4 = pink

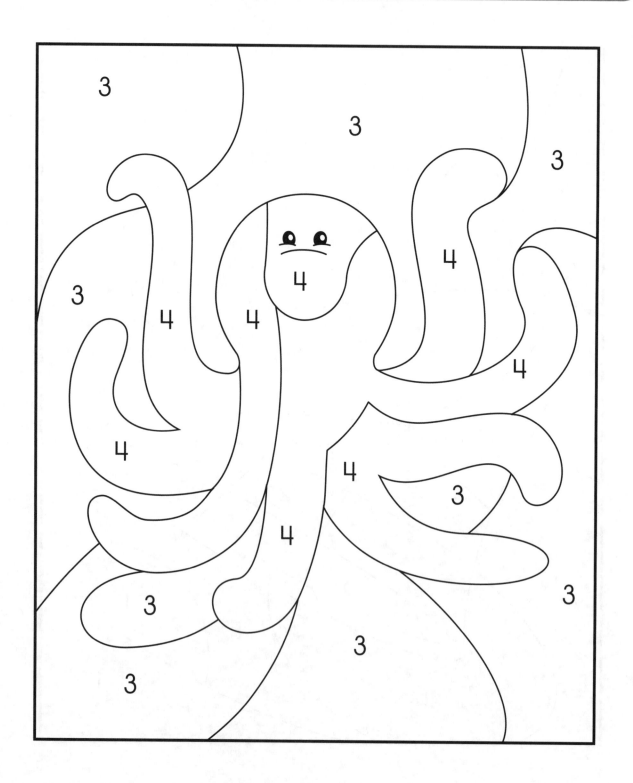

Hidden Picture

Use the code to color the spaces and find the hidden picture.

5 = **brown**   6 = **blue**   7 = yellow   8 = **red**

Hidden Picture

Use the code to color the spaces and find the hidden picture.

7 = **gray**   8 = **orange**   9 = **green**

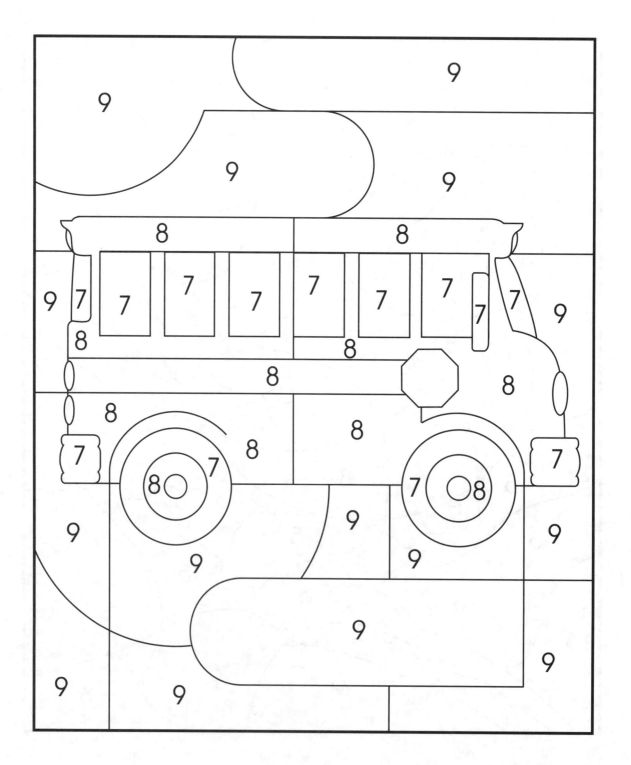

Hidden Picture

Use the code to color the spaces and find the hidden picture.

7 = **gray**   8 = **purple**   9 = yellow

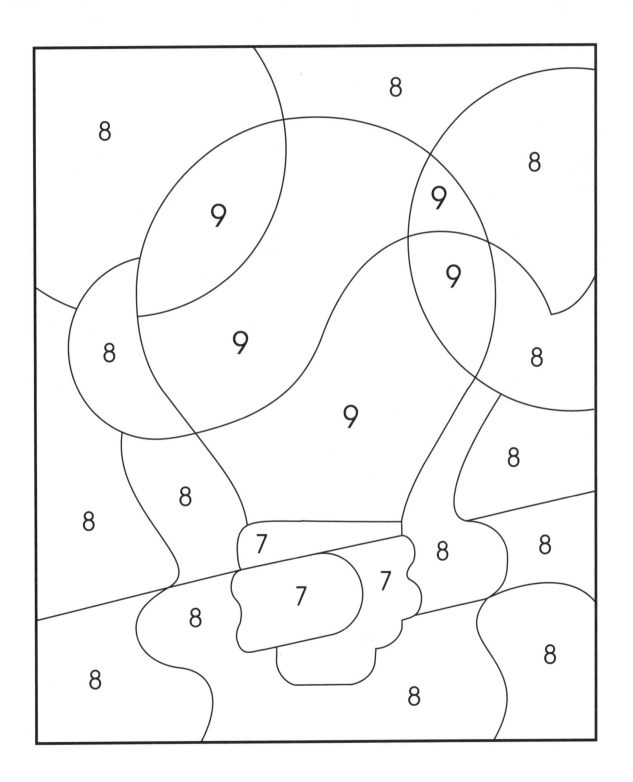

Hidden Picture

Use the code to color the spaces and find the hidden picture.

1 = **green**   2 = **purple**   3 = **blue**
4 = orange   5 = **red**

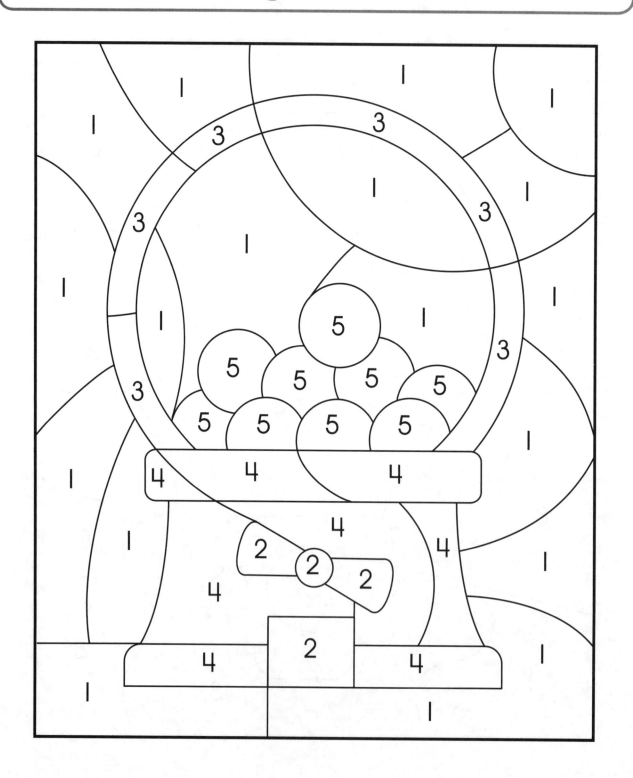

Hidden Picture

Use the code to color the spaces and find the hidden picture.

1 = **purple**   2 = **blue**   3 = **yellow**   4 = **red**

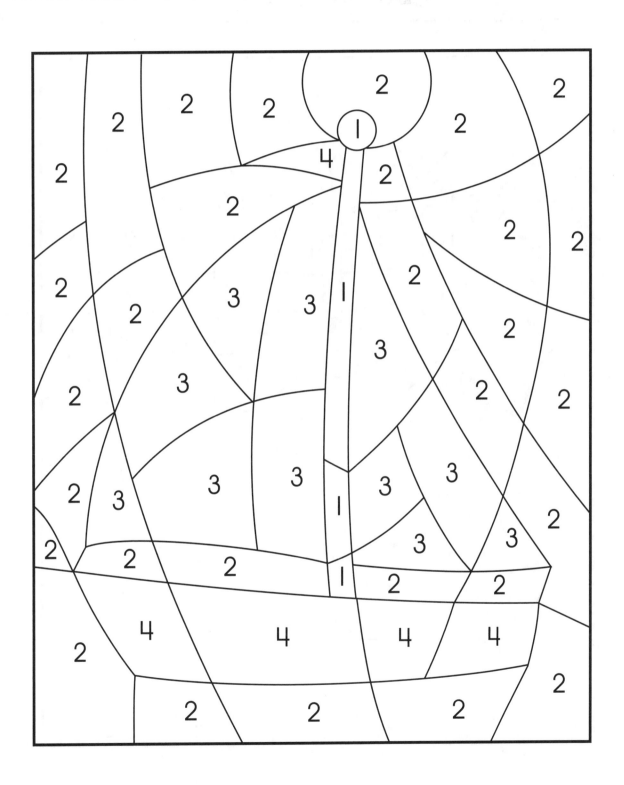

Hidden Picture

Use the code to color the spaces and find the hidden picture.

5 = **green**	6 = pink	7 = **blue**
8 = **brown**	9 = yellow	

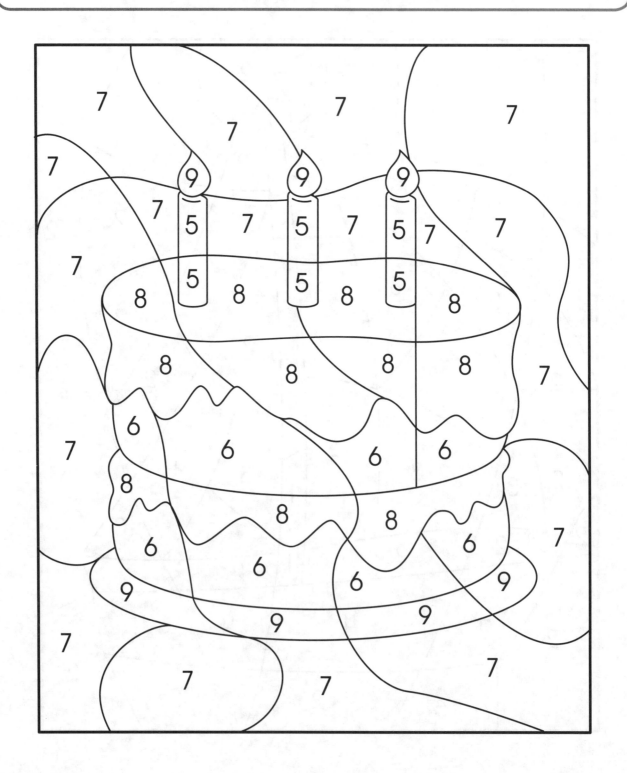

Dot-to-Dot 0-5

Connect the dots from 0 to 5. Start at the ★. Color the picture.

Dot-to-Dot 0-5

Connect the dots from 0 to 5. Start at the ★. Color the picture.

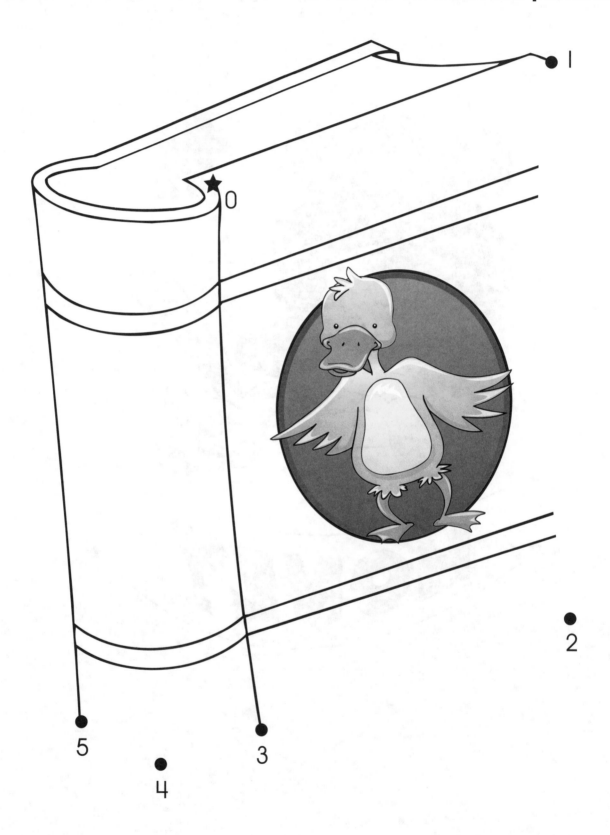

Dot-to-Dot 0-5

Connect the dots from 0 to 5. Start at the ★. Color the picture.

Dot-to-Dot 0-5

Connect the dots from 0 to 5. Start at the ★. Color the picture.

Dot-to-Dot 0-5

Connect the dots from 0 to 5. Start at the ★. Color the picture.

Dot-to-Dot 0-10

Connect the dots from 0 to 10. Start at the ★. Color the picture.

Dot-to-Dot 0-10

Connect the dots from 0 to 10. Start at the ★. Color the picture.

Dot-to-Dot 0-10

Connect the dots from 0 to 10. Start at the ★. Color the picture.

Dot-to-Dot 0-10

Connect the dots from 0 to 10. Start at the ★. Color the picture.

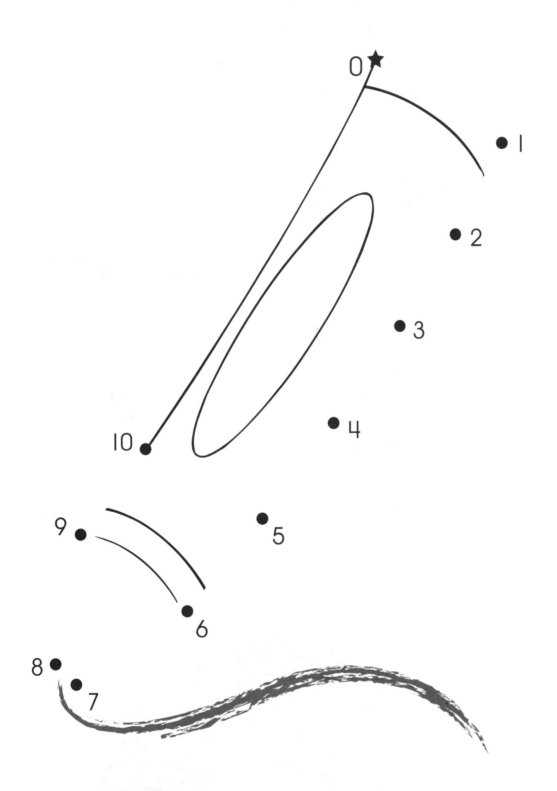

Dot-to-Dot 0-10

Connect the dots from 0 to 10. Start at the ★. Color the picture.

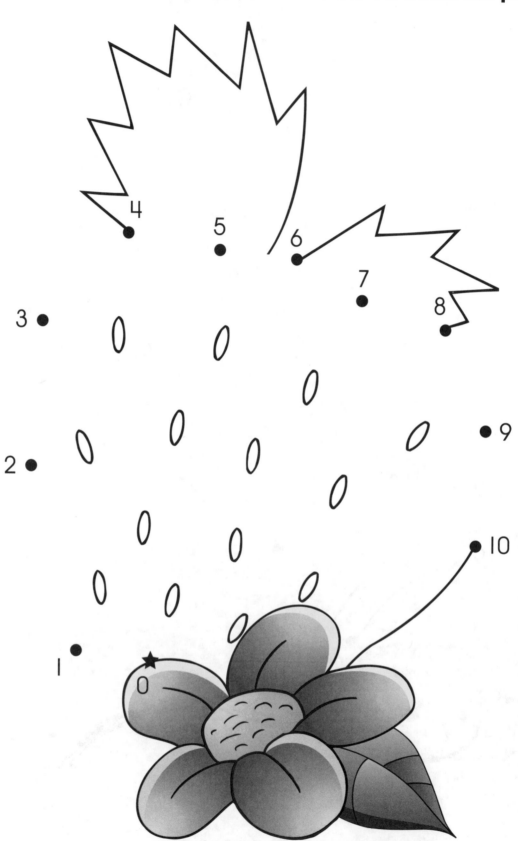

204

Dot-to-Dot 0-15

Connect the dots from 0 to 15. Start at the ★. Color the picture.

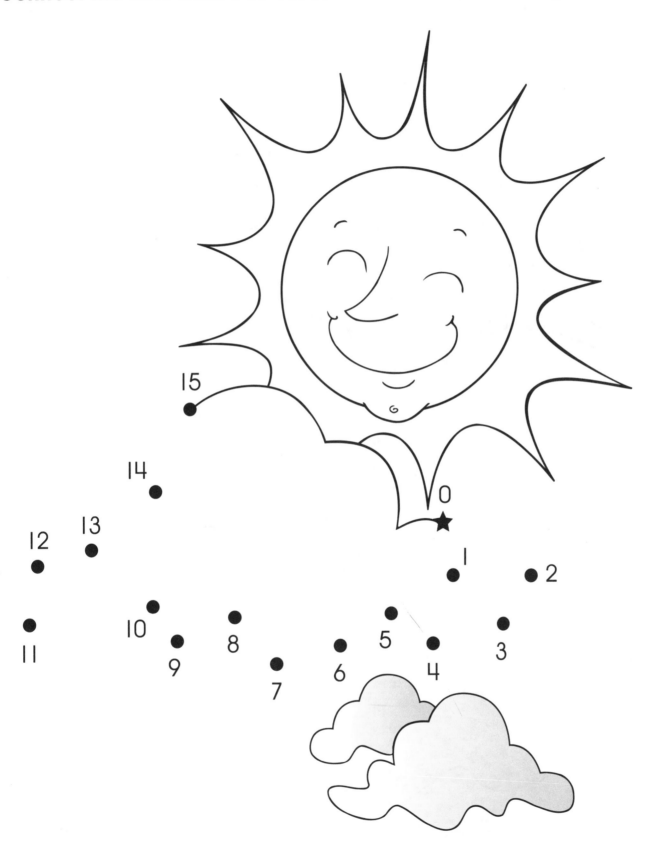

Dot-to-Dot 0-15

Connect the dots from 0 to 15. Start at the ★. Color the picture.

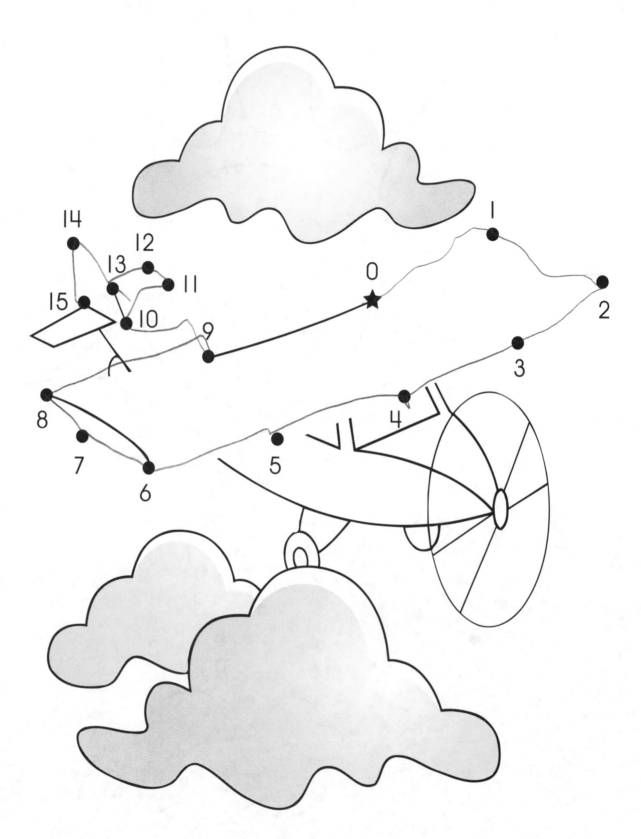

Dot-to-Dot 0-15

Connect the dots from 0 to 15. Start at the ★. Color the picture.

Dot-to-Dot 0-15

Connect the dots from 0 to 15. Start at the ★. Color the picture.

Dot-to-Dot 0-15

Connect the dots from 0 to 15. Start at the ★. Color the picture.

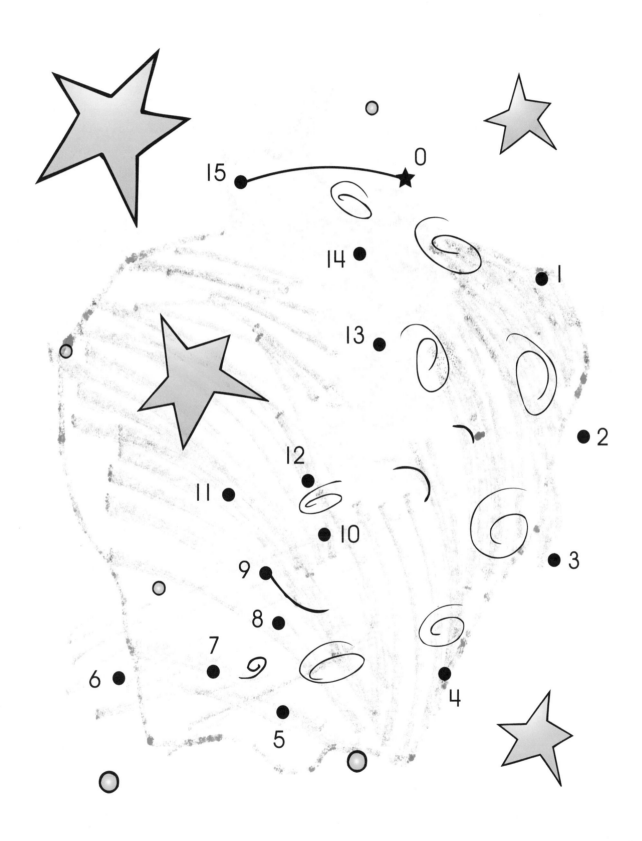

Dot-to-Dot 0-15

Connect the dots from 0 to 15. Start at the ★. Color the picture.

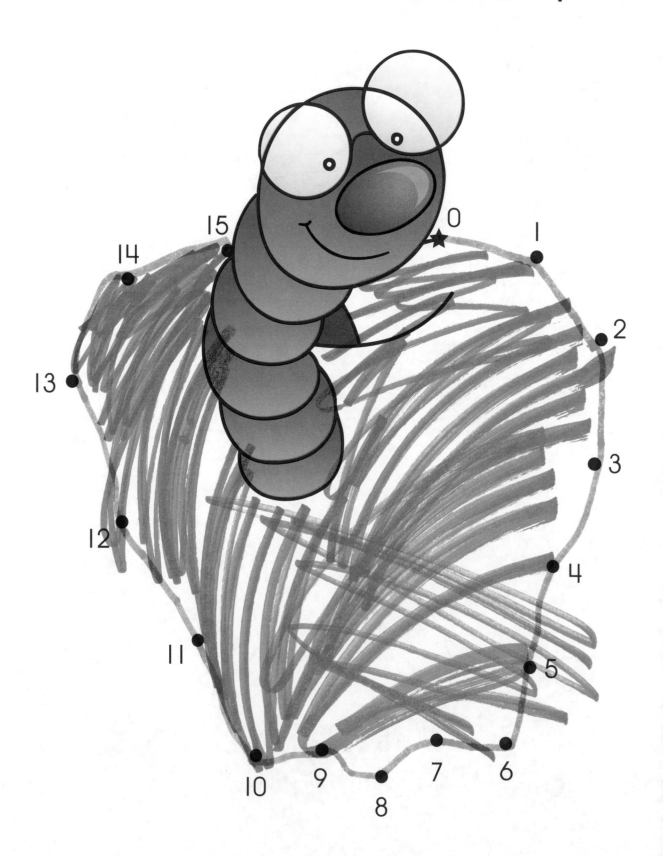

Dot-to-Dot 0-20

Connect the dots from 0 to 20. Start at the ★. Color the picture.

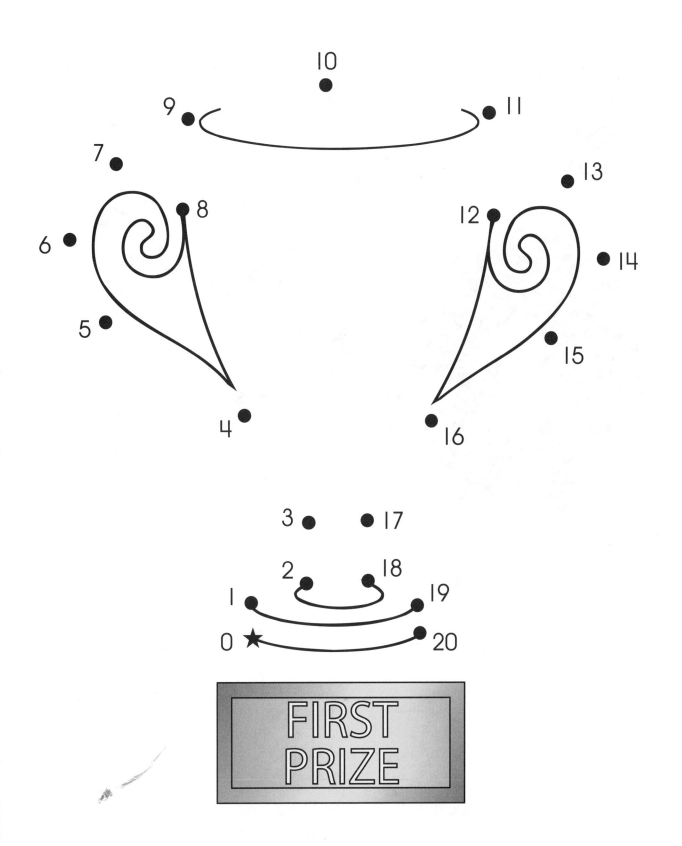

Dot-to-Dot 0-20

Connect the dots from 0 to 20. Start at the ★. Color the picture.

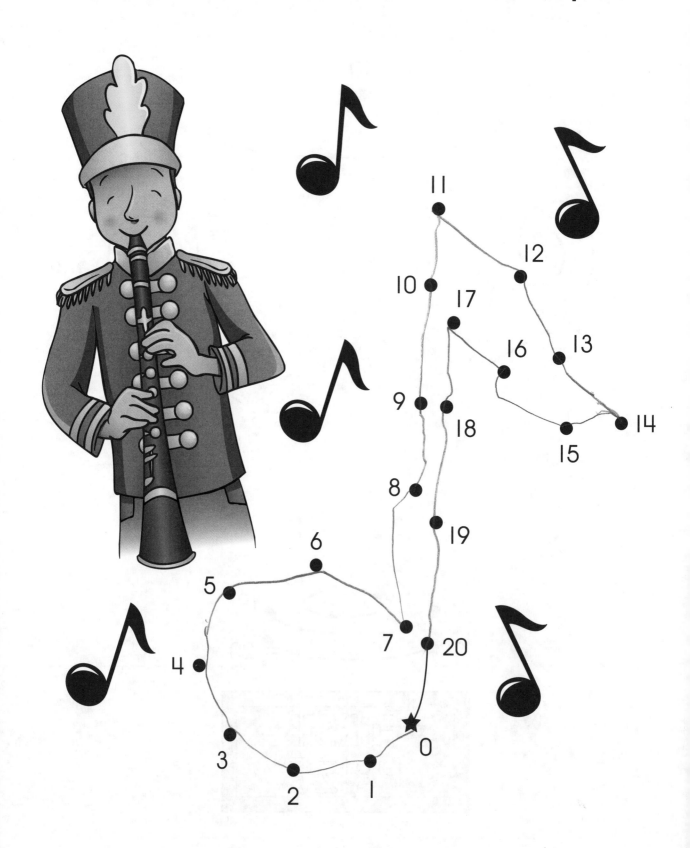

Dot-to-Dot 0-20

Connect the dots from 0 to 20. Start at the ★. Color the picture.

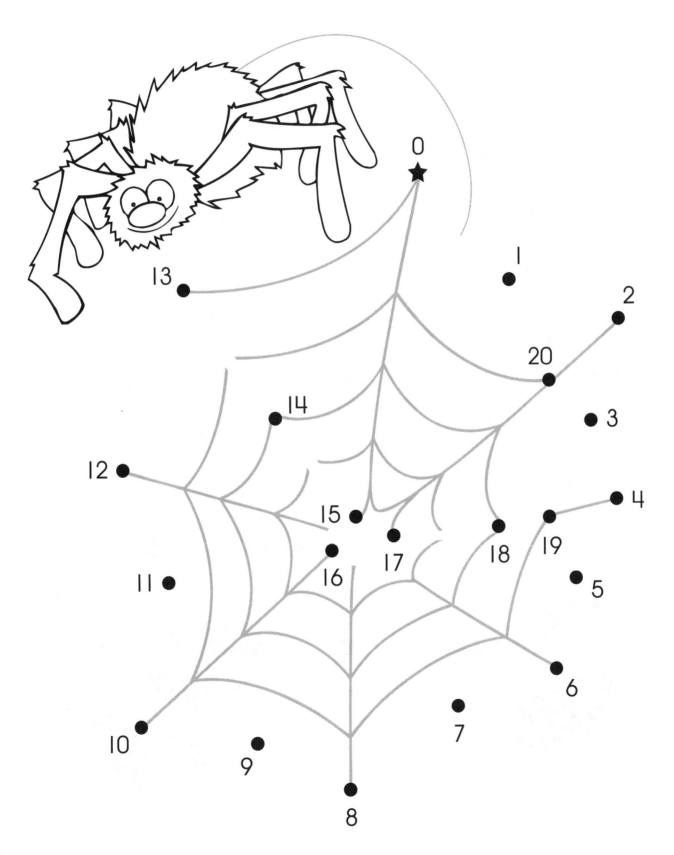

Dot-to-Dot 0-20

Connect the dots from 0 to 20. Start at the ★. Color the picture.

Dot-to-Dot 0-20

Connect the dots from 0 to 20. Start at the ★. Color the picture.

Dot-to-Dot 0-20

Connect the dots from 0 to 20. Start at the ★. Color the picture.

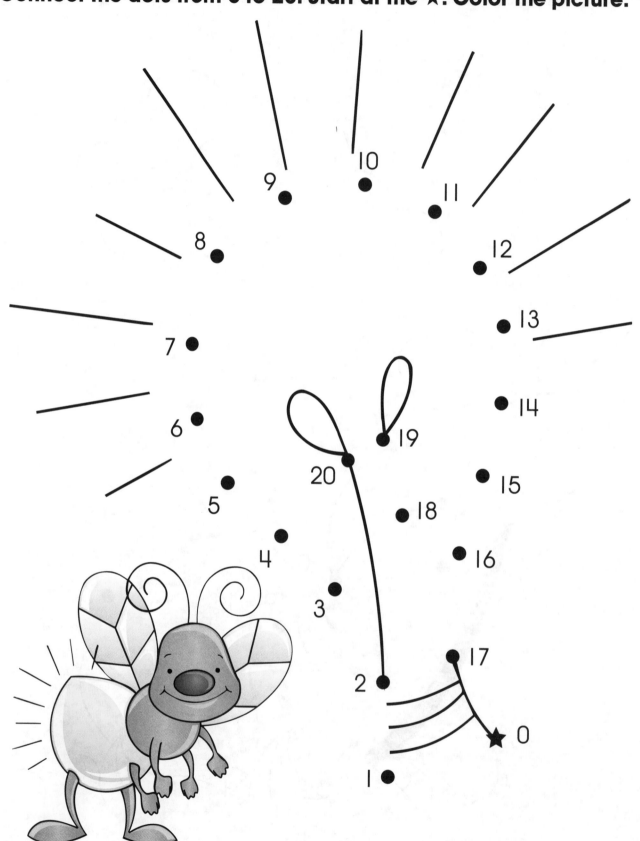

Dot-to-Dot 0-25

Connect the dots from 0 to 25. Start at the ★. Color the picture.

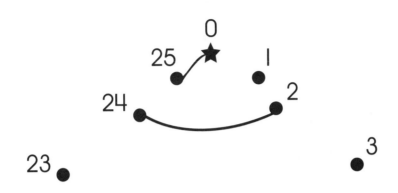

0
25
1
24
2
23
3
22
4
21
5
20
6
19
7
18
8
17
9
16
10
15
11
14
12
13

Dot-to-Dot 0-25

Connect the dots from 0 to 25. Start at the ★. Color the picture.

Dot-to-Dot O-25

Connect the dots from 0 to 25. Start at the ★. Color the picture.

Dot-to-Dot 0-25

Connect the dots from 0 to 25. Start at the ★. Color the picture.

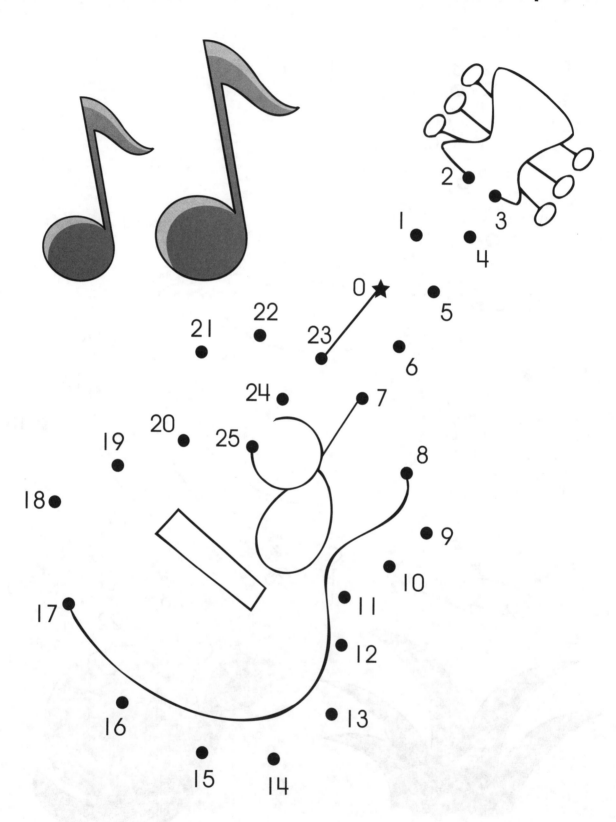

Dot-to-Dot 0-25

Connect the dots from 0 to 25. Start at the ★. Color the picture.

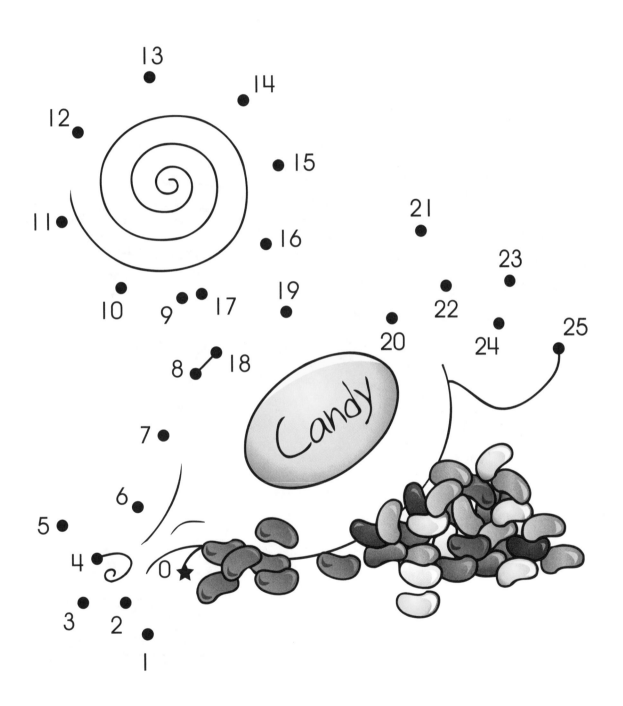

Dot-to-Dot 5-15

Connect the dots from 5 to 15. Start at the ★. Color the picture.

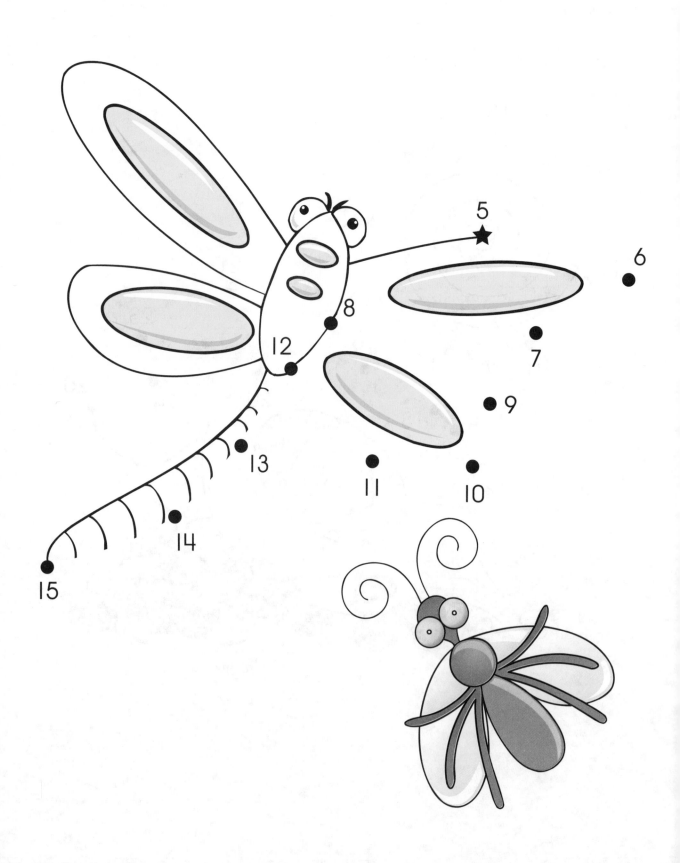

Dot-to-Dot 5-20

Connect the dots from 5 to 20. Start at the ★. Color the picture.

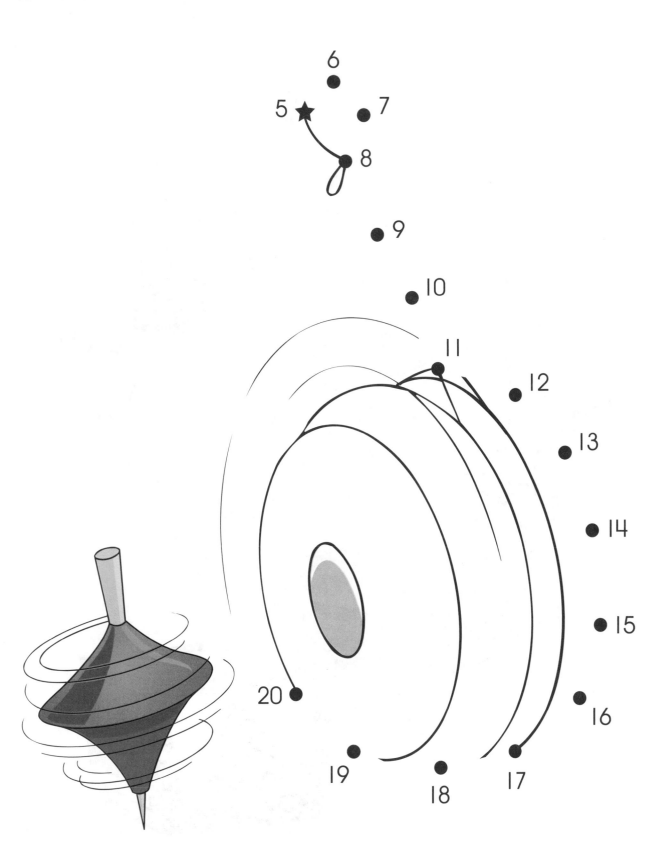

Dot-to-Dot 10-20

Connect the dots from 10 to 20. Start at the ★. Color the picture.

Dot-to-Dot 10-25

Connect the dots from 10 to 25. Start at the ★. Color the picture.

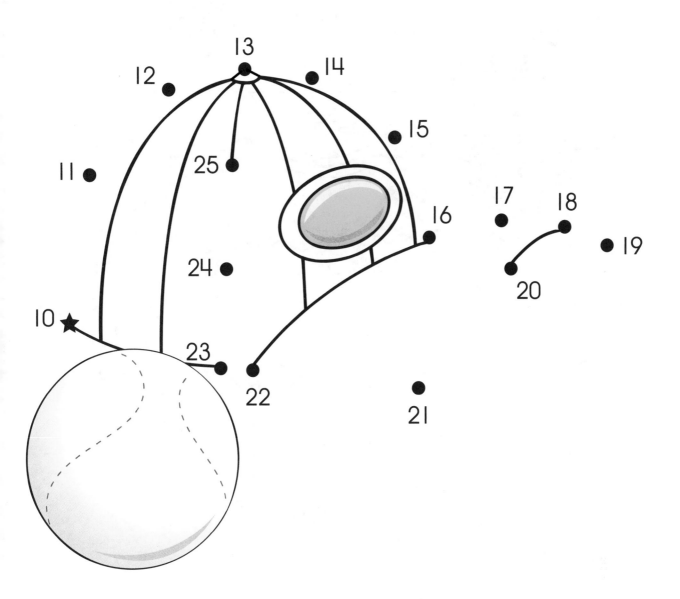

Maze

Follow the path to help the ship find the dock. Color the picture.

Maze

Follow the path to help the ant find the flowers.

Maze

Follow the path to help the snowplow clear the way to school.

Maze

Follow the path through the turtle's shell.

Maze

Follow the path to help the groundhog leave its burrow.

Maze

Follow the path to help the boy reach his cat. Color the picture.

Maze

Follow the path to help the boy race to the finish line.

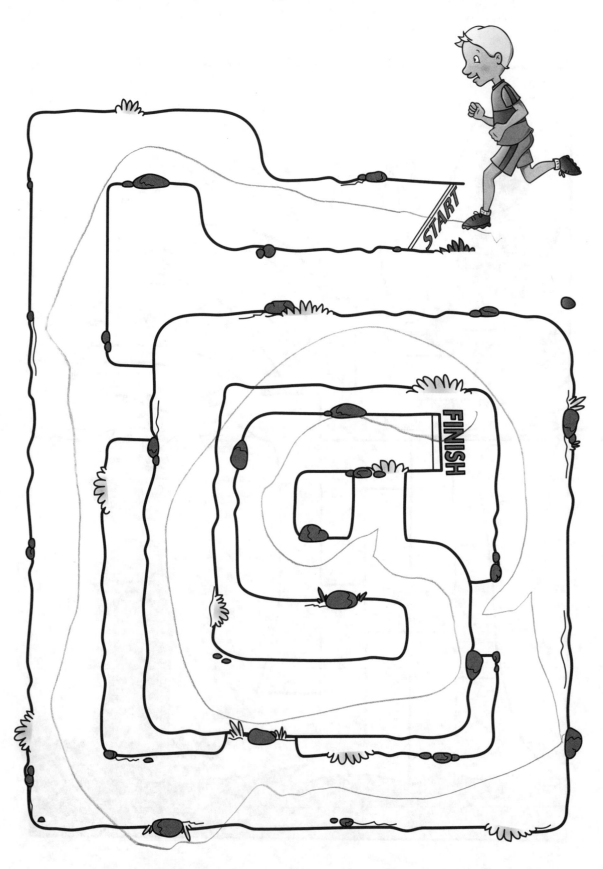

Maze

Follow the path to help the girl find her umbrella.

Maze

Follow the path to help the ants carry their lunch to the table.

Maze

Follow the path around the ladybug's spots.

Maze

Follow the path to help the airplane fly to the airport.

Maze

Follow the path through the snail's shell. Color the picture.

Maze

Follow the path to help the rocket fly to the moon.

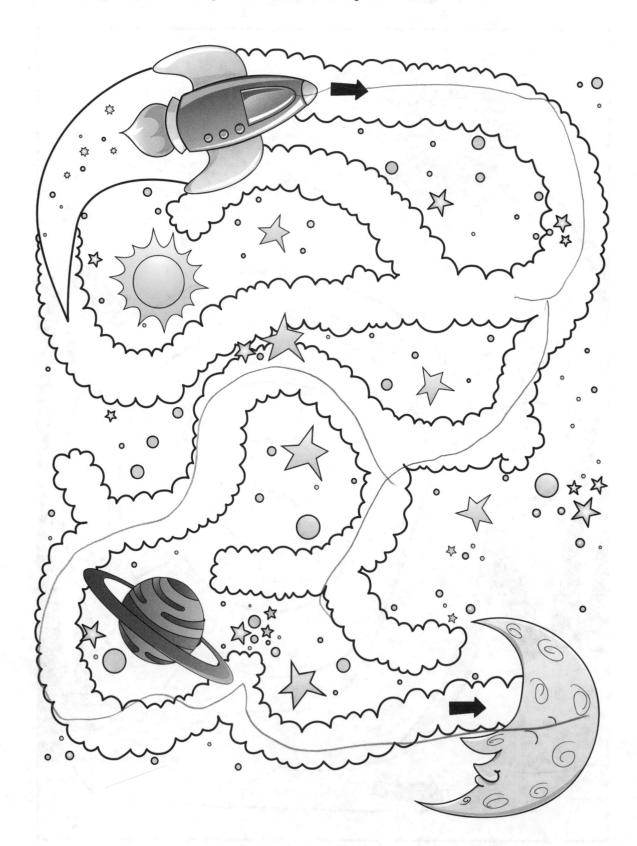

Maze

Follow the path to help the penguin find its friends.

Maze

Follow the path through the fish.

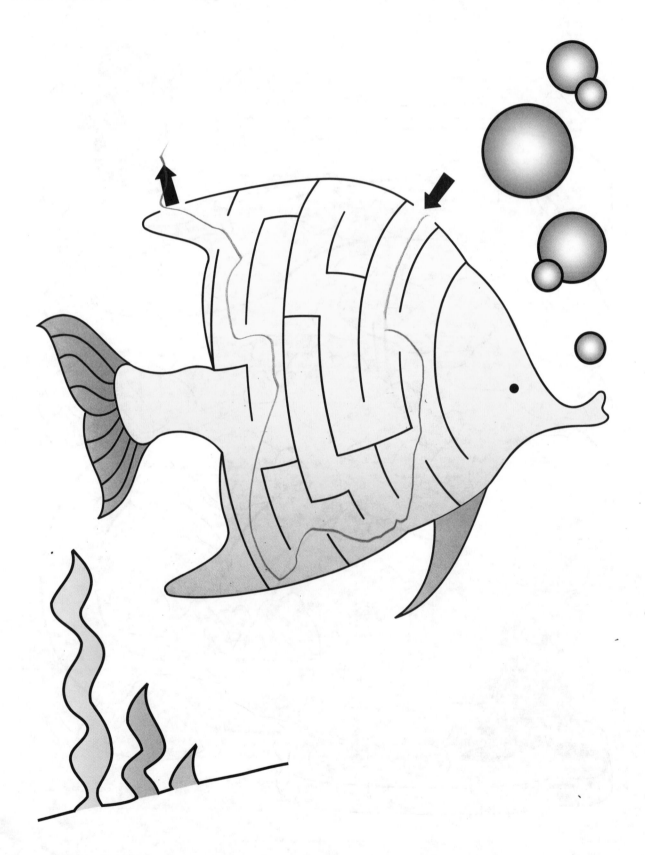

Maze

Follow the tracks to help the train find the tunnel.

Maze

Use a crayon to follow the path from the honey to the bear.

Maze

Follow the path to help the turtle swim to the log. Color the picture.

Maze

Follow the path through the ice cream sundae. Color the picture.

Maze

Use a crayon to follow the path from the boy to the butterfly.

Maze

Follow the path to help the bear find the biggest shell. Color the picture

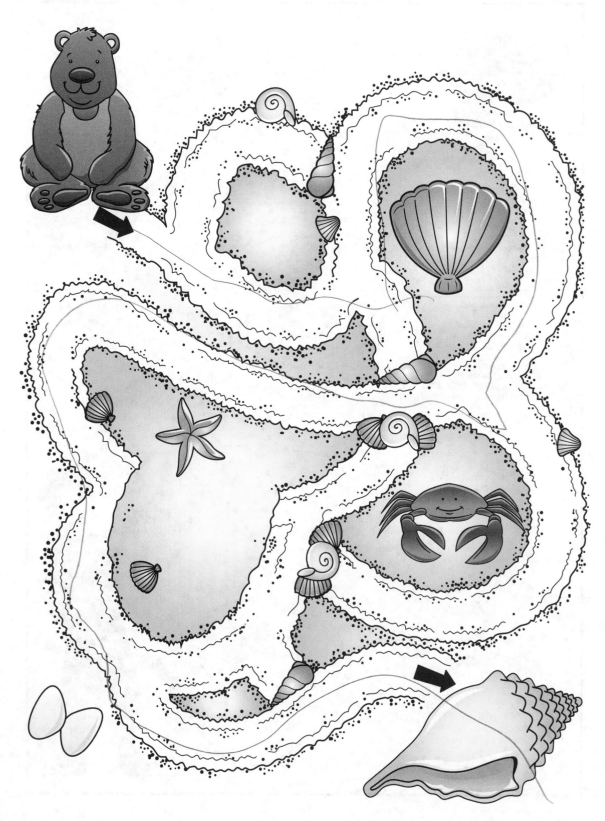

Maze

Follow the path to help the doe find her fawn. Color the picture.

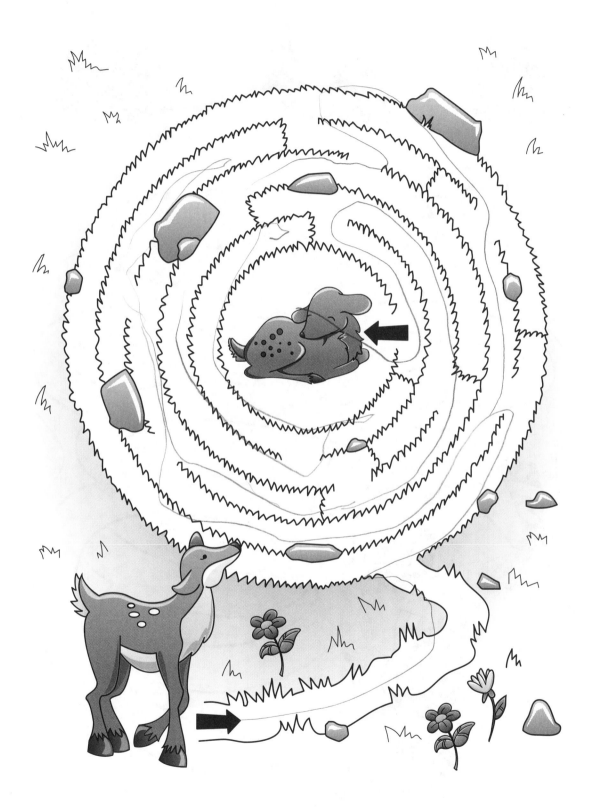

Maze

Follow the path to help the penguin score a goal.

Maze

Follow the path to help the girl find the sunken treasure. Color the picture.

Maze

Follow the path to help the girl find her tree house.

Maze

Trace each leash with a different colored crayon to find out who owns each dog.

Maze

Follow the path to help the rabbit find its easel.

Maze

Follow the path to help the pig find her piglets.

Maze

Follow the path to help the doll find the toy box.

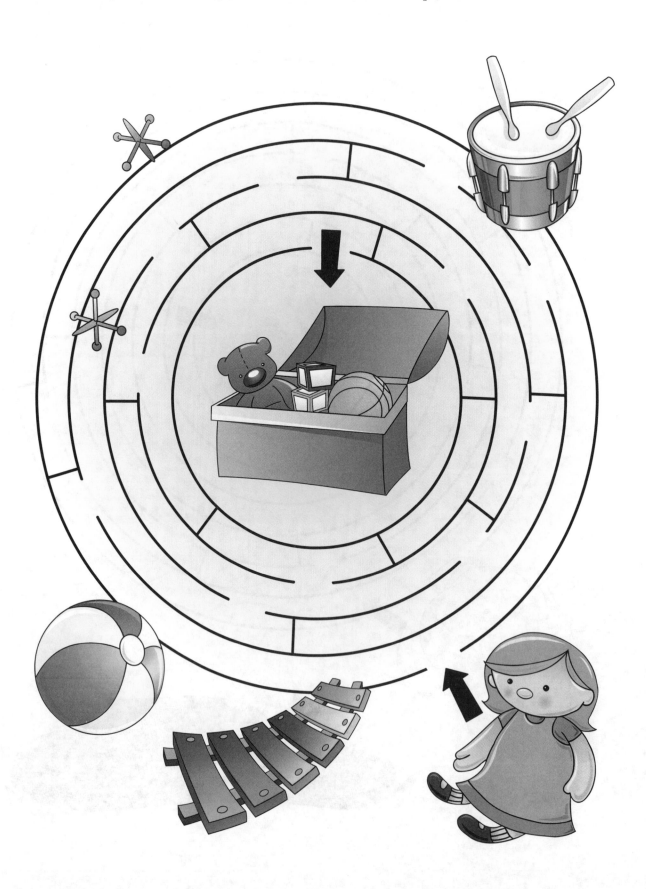

Maze

Trace each fishing line with a different colored crayon to find out who caught each fish.

Maze

Follow the path through the elephant. Color the picture.